THE MODERN CITY:
PLANNING IN THE 19TH CENTURY

PLANNING AND CITIES
(titles published to date)

PLANNING AND CITIES

General Editor

GEORGE R. COLLINS, Columbia University

THE MODERN CITY: PLANNING IN THE 19TH CENTURY

FRANÇOISE CHOAY

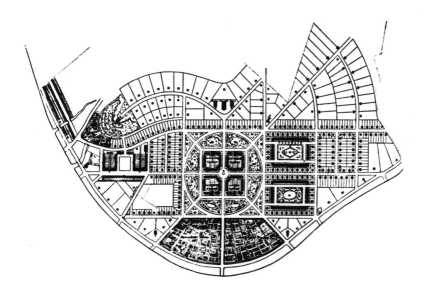

GEORGE BRAZILLER   NEW YORK

Translated by Marguerite Hugo and George R. Collins

© 1969 George Braziller, except in U.S.A.
All rights reserved
For information address the publisher:
George Braziller, Inc. 60 Madison Avenue New York, N.Y. 10010
Standard Book Number: 0-8076-0520-4
Library of Congress Catalog Card Number: 77-90408
Book design by Jennie Bush
Jacket design by Toshihiro Katayama
Printed in the United States of America
Fifth Printing, 1989

CONTENTS

GENERAL EDITOR'S PREFACE

Although we face unique urban problems in our day, many of the strengths and weaknesses of our present cities have been inherited directly from the nineteenth century. Much has been written about the impact of the Industrial Revolution on urban centers, so Françoise Choay is inevitably dealing with many familiar issues in this book. Her analysis of nineteenth-century theory and practice with respect to the regularization and planning of cities has, however, a novelty about it which should permit us to see the accomplishments and frustrations of that century in a different light than usual.

This volume is part of a series of books on cities and planning. It is our intention to deal with a number of epochs, areas, theoretical positions, and individual planners. While the emphasis is on the physical condition or design of towns and cities, we have tried to enlist authors who are concerned with the social, economic, and political forces that are essential to an understanding of architectural and urban form.

It is our hope that a series of concise, illustrated volumes on various aspects of cities and planning will, by the very different attitudes and assumptions of our several authors, fulfill a need and provide a complement to the more encyclopedic survey books that exist in various languages on the history of architectural city planning.

G.R.C.

THE CRITICAL ORDER

> We are essentially children of the 19th century, however
> passionate our revolts or disavowals, however profound our
> discouragement. *Fernand Braudel*[1]

The terms *urbanización, urbanisme, town-planning, Städtebau,*
which are used today to designate indiscriminately all forms of
city planning from ancient to modern, were, in fact, formulated
for the first time during the second half of the nineteenth
century. Originally they were intended to mark, with the full
impact of a neologism, the advent of an entirely novel relationship between Western man and the organization of his cities—
resulting from the Industrial Revolution. When Ildefonso Cerdá
coined the word *urbanización* in 1867, he meant it to define a
new field of activity, as yet "intact, virgin,"[2] for which the Spanish language had no appropriate term.

This mental attitude toward planning is still true in the
twentieth century, but familiarity with the word urbanism has
caused us to forget the original impulse that the term represented
historically. Therefore, before we can consider the various forms
which this new process assumed in the nineteenth century, the
specific nature of the process itself must be determined and
comparisons must be drawn with previous attitudes in order to
show the extent to which it represented a mutation.

Until the Industrial Revolution, the urban complex may have
been a semiotic system,[3] whose elements were related syn-
chronically within the context of rules and a code practiced by
inhabitant and planner alike. By virtue of its relationship with
all the other social systems (political power, learning, economy,
religion), the urban system asserted itself as one of communication and information. In other words, the citizen in the process
of inhabiting his city is integrated into the structure of a given
society at a specific moment in time, and every plan that might
exist corresponds implicitly to that structure which it both
institutes and controls. For example, in a given medieval German
town, the urban order—mainly syntagmatic,[4] i.e., the relationship of contiguity dominating—is related to church, feudal
system and corporate artisanship. The form of an individual
house and its position along the ribbon of the street situated
its occupant with relation to the dual transcendence of the
cathedral (the clock tower marked the hours of his life) and the
castle—and at the same time individualized him within a
community of secular tasks. Every urban plan was a direct
projection of the objectives of clergy, feudal lord or merchant
guild.

During the Baroque period, the urban order no longer had this all-inclusive significance; the role given in Baroque planning to the satisfaction of the eye destroys the former sense of intimacy, and the city is transformed into a spectacle. Nonetheless, the radial avenues, as well as the vantage points where they originated and where they terminated, were still designed with reference to the established power, although in a new form, at the same time as they incorporated the knowledge of the period—since Baroque esthetics cannot be understood when disconnected from contemporary science. Vauban and Le Nôtre were at once the King's planners and the disciples of Galileo and Descartes. In short, the relationship between the urban system and other concurrent systems was still implicitly accepted by both inhabitant and planner.

The Industrial Revolution brings about a radical transformation. It is accompanied by a spontaneous and unprecedented urbanization which presents two faces. On the one hand new agglomerations are formed, on a gridiron plan—particularly in the United States; meanwhile the Old World experiences an upheaval in her ancient towns which revolutionizes not only *the spatial organization*, but also the mentality of the *city dweller* and the *initiative of the planner*.

The alteration in spatial organization is brought about both by the filling and the overflow of the former city limits[5] and by the division of the town into two antagonist groups that correspond to the production-consumption dichotomy.[6] From 1830 to 1900 the population of London doubled, jumping from two to four million inhabitants. The population of Paris rose from one million to more than two, and that of Berlin, 150,000 at the start of the century, had reached 1,300,000 by the 1890's. Concurrently, a sharp division was created between peripheral areas of factories and manufacturing and the central business districts where stock exchanges were installed, banks multiplied, large stores and hotels appeared. "The cellar population of the working people"[7] began to cluster in central or peripheral *slums* as opposed to the *expensive residential districts* to which the city's high-income groups were migrating.

As for the city dweller, he was unable to assimilate this urban revolution in terms of any previous process in which one urban order was blotted out by another. The situation had become dramatic, for he was now confronted with a spatial order devoid of its traditional richness of meaning. It had become monosemantical in the sense that its organization derived solely from the economic cause of its high demographic concentration: capitalist-industrialist production. Three factors combine to explain this semantic impoverishment:

8

1) the virulence of the economic drive.

2) the fact that the urban community was profoundly disturbed by the irruption of extraneous immigrants from the country, alien to the significance and functioning of the city's institutions, in particular its spatial organization.

3) the development of increasingly abstract means of communication; the continuity of rooted communication is replaced by new systems which continue to perfect themselves throughout the nineteenth century, allowing the population greater mobility and providing information that is more precisely synchronized with the accelerating rhythm of history. Railway, daily press and telegraph will gradually supplant *space* in its previous informative and formative role.

This process, both qualitative and quantitative, is the basis of a new relationship with respect to the urban complex. Following the loss of partial conscious control and of implicit subconscious control, those actually experiencing the urban phenomenon came to consider it as something alien. They no longer felt inside the process and determined by it; they remained outside, observing the transformation with the eye of the spectator. The inhabitant suddenly saw the city as transformed by that "incidence of strangeness," which Claude Lévi-Strauss considers the prerequisite of ethnological observation. Furthermore, this attitude that the city is something subject to examination has been made possible by a simultaneous evolution in the structure of knowledge. Since the end of the eighteenth century, Western man has begun to view the entirety of his material and spiritual productions with a certain objectivity. Historical perspective provided the necessary dimension for the analysis of them and helped elaborate the new concepts of labor, economics, and art. At the beginning of the nineteenth century, conditions were therefore ripe for the advent of a new study of man through the social sciences. True, only at the end of the century did sociology become a theoretical science, but sociological description appeared with the industrial city— which proved to be its favorite subject.

The nineteenth century has its monuments of urban sociology: the works of social reformers like Edwin Chadwick or of Great Britain's Royal Investigations Commissions and Select Committees; the social research of ideologists like Frédéric Le Play; Engels' polemical synthesis in *Die Lage der arbeitenden Klasse;* and the descriptions of social novelists like Mrs. Gaskell, Dickens,[8] Zola, or Eugène Süe. Here the urban phenomenon is not yet observed with the statistician's cold eye, as it will be toward the end of the century; but it is viewed for the first time with a *clinical eye*. To these writers the semantic loss of the urban phenomenon and the transition from partial control in urban development to an absence of control, with its concomitant sanitation problems, makes them view the urban agglomeration as a diseased condition, or worse, a monstrous deformity. Hence the creation of new metaphors evoking the city as a chancre, a cancer, a leprous body.[9] In less colorful terms the upheaval will be described as chaos, disorder. In 1844, Engels described the "urban mess" of British industrial cities and to a journalist writing in 1856, London seems "the result of a gigantic accident."[10] "Big cities...formless masses, jumbles of houses... architectural chaos," wrote Victor Considérant in 1858.[11]

Such scandalous "disorder"—a new reality—calls for a new type of planning on the part of the *planner*. The process of urban organization at this point loses its original immediacy, as it now evolves about an object that has been removed from its context by analysis; for the first time the umbilical cord has been cut, so to speak, and the city subjected to critical examination. Consequently, the planning which was to emerge specifically from this critical approach may be termed *critical planning*. Its birthplace will be the old town, since the checkerboard layout of new cities was adapted to the requirements of industrial society and provoked only a partial or delayed critical reaction.

During the nineteenth century critical planning will take three forms, best defined as *regularization*, *pre-urbanism*, and *urbanism*. These, however, include only that fraction of nineteenth-century projects and experiments consciously related to the capitalist-industrialist phase. They must be differentiated from the many previous or contemporary projects and achievements which were to carry on the pre-critical tradition throughout the century. The persistence of the latter can be explained by the complex chronology of the Industrial Revolution, and in the case of Great Britain, by the permanence of her old social structures, which no revolution was able to shatter.

Although the transformation in Western man's mental processes and conceptual tools already began during the last decades of the eighteenth century, and although major technical developments had then taken place—between 1765 and 1774 Watt developed the steam engine and in 1785 Cartwright invented the mechanical loom—it was not until 1806 that the first large cotton mill opened in Manchester. And even as late as 1830 the cotton industry was practically the only one mechanized; in the world's leading industrial country the structure of artisanal labor had remained unchanged. In Europe and the United States, the scales did not tip in favor of the industrial system until the forties, with the development of a new form of communication, the railway. The railway is the major technical invention that brought into play the new forms of production and promoted the growth of large urban concentrations. From 1840 on, railway and capitalism were to develop hand in hand, and having weathered the crises of the years around 1848, the "railways became the new economy's most powerful weapon," causing the new urban type to prevail.

The date 1851, year of the Great Exhibition in London, is a significant one. From then on England is the first country to establish official criteria for differentiating between rural and urban areas. By then, half of Great Britain's population is urban. However, the mutation will not be complete until the 1870's; for a long period of time the structure of urban real estate helped maintain the old spatial order. With respect to Great Britain, which remained the leader until the 1880's, the European countries like Italy or Spain will have to wait almost until the twentieth industrial phase with varying time lags. "The development of their respective railways reveals the age of their economies."[12] Countries like Italy or Spain will have to wait almost until the twentieth century before an industrial order is established.

For these reasons, throughout the entire nineteenth century one witnesses the creation, extension, or organization of cities along three para- or pre-industrial patterns:

1) the Baroque or Neoclassical ceremonial form;
2) the essentially British residential pattern;
3) the colonial checkerboard schema.

The Baroque and Neoclassical form with its monuments, its broad avenues lined with uniform buildings, its parks, its love for vistas and geometry, remained meaningful until the 1830's, deteriorating into formalism only toward the end of the century. It continued to be used in the creation, extension and embellishment of cities (*Fig. 1*).

Thus Washington was built on the plan of L'Enfant (1756–1825), with modifications which altered its logic but not its profound meaning. And in 1806, Woodward proposed a plan for Detroit which was based on the same esthetic principles. So around the old cities of Europe, between the ancient walls and the later bastions, suburbs and new towns of the eighteenth century continue to develop as in Berlin (*Fig. 2*). In Bremen (*Figs. 3–4*), Lubeck, Cologne, Vienna (*Fig. 5*) and Cracow, seventeenth-century fortifications that had become useless owing to modern artillery were transformed into promenades and gardens, but the formal esthetic of their design was not modified. Though the meaning of the word had been altered, the structure of the language remained unchanged. This was equally true within the city proper. In France, Napoleon I was the "executor of the Old Régime's will,"[13] and his urban projects were designed essentially to embellish the city. Thus the first section of the rue de Rivoli was opened up in 1806 with the rue de la Paix, rue de Castiglione and rue des Pyramides as side-streets; uniform houses with arcades were constructed along the rue de Rivoli and rue des Pyramides, the intention being to please the eye and complete the Baroque composition stretching from the Tuileries to the Etoile, which Louis XV had dreamt of extending from the Place du Trône (*Fig. 6*).

Also Baroque were Antolini's projects for Milan and Berthault's for the Pincio in Rome. In Great Britain the archetypal image remained the eighteenth-century masterpiece, Bath, with its Circus and its crescents displaying identical facades. John Nash (1752–1835) was to be inspired by Bath—as well as by the rue de Rivoli—in his project for Regent Street (1812–1819) (*Fig. 7*), the royal ceremonial way that was designed for the pleasure of the Prince of Wales, to connect Portland Place and Carlton House (*Fig. 9*). And in Vienna, the Imperial power as embodied in Franz-Josef, faithfully maintained the ideals of classical planning. By 1858, due to the effects of industrialization on the capital, the Ring had become a practical necessity, but it was nevertheless invaded by monuments and structured in accordance with esthetic requirements (*Fig. 8*).

In English cities the residential pattern was conditioned by standards and a system of practical and esthetic values which had been established in the seventeenth century and were to remain effective and unchanged until the end of Victoria's reign.[14] Evidence of this is found in London, in the Bloomsbury districts, Mayfair, Belgravia, Regent's Park (*Figs. 9–10*). From Covent Garden, for which Inigo Jones (1572–1651) received the commission in 1630 from the fourth Earl of Bedford, to Bedford Square (1776), Tavistock Square (1864) or Gordon Square (1860), the principles of layout are the same (*Figs. 10–11*). This specifically British form of planning was the work of the great landlords and an outgrowth of the particular status of land tenure in some English cities, notably London. The great land-holding families, whose rural estates surrounded the towns and could be used for urban expansion, retained ownership of their property, while renting to building contractors. From the seventeenth to the nineteenth centuries leases were gradually extended from thirty to sixty, then to eighty and ninety-nine years, with increasingly restrictive and detailed clauses pertaining to rental or building.[15]

The latent and protracted control which the landowners

exercised over the operation of their *contractors* explains at once the merits and the shortcomings of this form of planning. On the one hand, landlords like the dukes of Bedford, St. Albans, or Westminster rented on a long-term basis and not for immediate profit, as their purpose was to "enhance the long-range value of their estate." As a result:

1) Unlike any contemporary civic plan, their transactions were organized and related over a period of time. (For this reason their building contracts have sometimes been described as "miniature town-planning."[16])

2) These operations were not conceived with an attitude of pomp or ceremony but for the more realistic and profitable purpose of housing.

3) They performed amply—at least for the upper classes—a certain function: residential developments were protected from contamination with labor operations of various types (trade, craft and industry) as well as from traffic; thus they flourished to one side of the main traffic arteries in an open fashion around rural elements that were carefully preserved in these so-called *squares*. Population density was limited, streets broadly designed, and the squares gave a meaning and focus around which to arrange the individual houses whose standardization permitted a maximum of comfort at the same time as they converted these residential areas into class communities. Steen Eiler Rasmussen compares the *square* to a garden in a convent.

4) Thanks to restoration and redevelopment, the spacious, airy character of these districts was maintained or improved upon so that when the upper classes abandoned them because they were no longer fashionable (this is what happened in Bloomsbury, for example, toward the 1830's), they were not allowed to deteriorate into slums.

On the other hand, since this form of hygienic and rational planning was motivated solely by the private interests of the individual landlord, the agglomeration as a whole was condemned to fragmentation. In the nineteenth century, London was really made up of nothing more than a number of dormitory villages juxtaposed around the City. Precautionary measures were incorporated into the plans for these communities, in order to ensure their autonomy and preserve their respectability. Thus in the 1830's, the property of the dukes of Bedford was covered with gates and barriers erected against invasion from the districts of the North. And Figs Mead (*Fig. 12*), for example, rented in 1834 for the creation of a "model suburb for the lower and lower middle classes," was protected from its slum neighbor, Somers' Town, by using a system of offset and diagonal roads instead of Somers' rectangular layout.[17] Furthermore, in most plans the number of openings was increased to the west, while to the east and north it was kept to a mimimum.

Amidst the chaos of the industrial era, the lovely residential neighborhoods of English cities seem to be symbols of order and humanism, which explains the enthusiastic praise they elicited from writers like Lewis Mumford or Steen Eiler Rasmussen. This should not make us forget, however, that planning of this type, born in the seventeenth century, is, in the nineteenth, no more than a relic, an anachronism.

Finally, the predominant urban pattern outside Europe was our third and last one—the colonial checkerboard—which can be associated with a variety of vocations and meanings. It assumed its most elementary form in the African military bases (Tlemcen, Orleansville) and its most elaborate in the cities of Latin America, where a network of public plazas, consecrated by Iberian tradition, was incorporated within the gridiron plan. In British dominions this pattern served administrative or political ends more and showed traces of Vitruvianism. Such was the case with Pretoria in South Africa (1835) and, in Australia, Adelaide which was designed by Light in 1837 (*Fig. 13*). In the United States mention should be made of the unusual example provided by Salt Lake City, which was founded in 1847 in accordance with a plan elaborated by Joseph Smith in 1833. Here the checkerboard corresponds to a religious order based on biblical geometry; the city's generative element is Temple Block (including Temple, Tabernacle, and Assembly), whose sides are oriented toward the four cardinal points of the compass (*Fig. 14*).

In other North American cities, this ancient form was applied only in urban fragments. The checkerboard was the elementary pattern of land division whether applied to virgin land or in extensions to older cities of European type. The latter is the case of New York, where expansion to the North, planned in 1811, gave rise to problems of connection—hence Washington Square, Madison Square and Union Square (*Fig. 15*). Semantically meagre, the gridiron pattern has no other meaning than that of an efficient tool. After serving colonizers, traders and gold seekers, it became the instrument of industrial capitalism, simultaneously available for speculation or traffic circulation.

The Baroque, the residential and the colonial patterns—three forms of urban planning in the nineteenth century— have been discussed here only incidentally. Though belonging chronologically to our period, they call into play preceding sociohistorical orders. Our sole concern in the following pages will be critical planning, whose originality will stand out more clearly in contrast to these briefly described systems. Our purpose is essentially to bring out the meaning and articulations of the new process which will be described through representative examples—ideal types—without an exhaustive examination of specific projects and their execution.

REGULARIZATION

We mean by *regularization*—a word borrowed from Haussmann —that form of critical planning whose explicit purpose is to regularize the disordered city, to disclose its new order by means of a pure, schematic layout which will disentangle it from its dross, the sediment of past and present failures.[18]

For the spontaneous urbanization of the industrial era the Old World had two types of cities to offer: the open city, like London, which was free for unlimited expansion, and the closed city, like Paris, bounded by ancient walls. It is not surprising that the most elaborate and precocious plan originated in an enclosed city, where the disorder created by spatial limitation was more shocking and hopeless. In spite of the fact that in 1850 France was economically behind Great Britain, Paris was the object of the first perfected plan for regularization of a city in the industrial age.

THE PLAN OF HAUSSMANN

The author of the transformation of Paris, Baron Georges Haussmann (1809–1891), Prefect of the Seine from 1853 to 1870, has been generally misunderstood. Of his undertaking in Paris, historians have frequently stressed the destruction that he inflicted on the city (*Figs. 16–17*). And the "vandalism" of this "Attila of the straight line"[19] has too often been interpreted as deference to Napoleon III's concern with matters of internal security: the Emperor wanted to put an end to riots by destroying the medieval structure of Parisian streets (*Figs. 18–19*) and replacing them with broad arteries along which the police could assemble and charge. It is true that Haussmann was a faithful servant of the Emperor. But the latter had more in mind than his personal security. He was preoccupied with social problems and eager to adjust his capital to a revolution whose significance and consequences he had become aware of during his exile in England. Moreover, if we compare Haussmann's scheme with earlier plans for the reorganization of Paris or if we consider the *Reports* he prepared while in office and the *Mémoires* he published at the end of his life, it is evident that being fundamentally an administrator,[20] he actually had little interest in politics. The scope of his vision far surpassed the Emperor's, and in this endeavor he was highly creative and original.

Haussmann's project cannot be explained simply as a matter of strategy or as a concern for improved sanitation—which produced the celebrated water and sewage systems. His initial objective stands in sharp and original contrast to contemporary projects; his purpose was to give unity to and to transform into an operative whole the "huge consumer market, the immense workshop"[21] of the Parisian agglomerate. In 1853, Paris was still a collection of juxtaposed parts whose particular characteristics were no longer meaningfully related to the viewpoint or behavior of an increasingly mobile and shifting population that was actuated by the capitalistic drive for accumulation of wealth. It had apparently never occurred to the successive authors of earlier plans that Paris as a whole, or simply the right or left banks, could one day become a single organism quickened with a unique life."[22]

Even when previous planning attempted to project far into the future, it remained fragmentary and governed above all by esthetic considerations. Analysis of the Artists' Plan, worked out in 1793 for the Convention, shows that planning was done by district (Fig. 20). It had essentially two aims: either the dividing up of property confiscated from the Church with a network of roads suitable for its further development or, whenever a monument seemed inviting, the creation around it of a formal system of radiating avenues. Thus, Saint Sulpice, the Observatory and the Val de Grâce constituted the Left Bank's three esthetic poles (Fig. 21). The Observatory, for example, gave rise to a star-shaped Baroque project whose only justification was its perspective effects as it did not actually connect any significant centers of activity. Haussmann simply disregarded this and focused on a point farther north—the junctions of boulevards Port-Royal and Montparnasse with the boulevard Saint-Michel (Fig. 23). From his point of view the problem of the Left Bank was both one of unification—to be achieved by opening wide throughways running in both directions—and one of organic connection to the Right Bank. Consequently, he was to open (among others) the boulevard de Latour-Maubourg as a continuation of avenue d'Antin, the boulevard Saint-Germain as a line of connection between the two key districts of Etoile and Bastille, and boulevard Saint-Michel as a direct continuation of boulevard Sébastapol.

The Artists' Plan (Fig. 20) and Haussmann's (Fig. 22) reflect two conceptions of the city. The first corresponds to the Paris of Balzac,[23] with its various societies enclosed within their separate quarters, while Haussmann's is the Paris of Zola, a metropolis unified by the fever of capitalism.

By and large, the now thoroughly familiar idea of the *big city* as a unified entity was still foreign to the mentality of Haussmann's period. In Great Britain, for example, the first official proposal for comprehensive treatment of the capital was not made until 1909, when John Burns introduced the Town Planning Bill.

Haussmann's method of attack was as original as his task. All decisions had first to be supported by analysis of the existing situation. His "initial studies" (to use the Prefect's own expression) are evidence against the a-priori reasoning of which he has been accused. He examined his object of study in relation to two coordinates—time and space—and his first step on entering the Hôtel de Ville was to have drawn up a detailed and accurate plan of the whole city, the first of its kind. This year-long operation included a planimetric survey by triangulation as well as a topographical survey.[24] When the surveys were completed, he had the plan engraved on large sheets, to the scale of 5/1000 (*Fig. 23*). The sheets were mounted on canvas and juxtaposed on a *frame on wheels*, forming a screen which never left his office. Haussmann constantly studied the plan, which complemented his firsthand knowledge of the city that had previously been acquired by covering "every inch" of Paris "on foot."

Haussmann's documentation was not static, however. The Prefect understood that a city, like any other organism, evolves in time, and that the view of the observer must therefore be at once prospective and retrospective, in order to safeguard its traditional dynamics as well as those orienting the future. How thoroughly he was acquainted with the capital's past may be judged from his summary of its history. It ranks for clarity with those of the best professional historians and enabled Haussmann to determine key zones and inert zones as well as those constants—the axes and poles—around which development occurs. Planning for the future would be facilitated by statistical data: like the present delegate of the Parisian District, Haussmann saw the future in terms of a population of millions of residents[25] and of economic needs increased millions of times.

On the basis of his analysis, by what means did the Prefect propose to achieve the efficient working unity of the city? Primarily through designing a circulatory system and opening a system of ventilation. Problems of traffic flow were given priority. Haussmann's first step was to conceive a network of through streets which have no significance in themselves but are essentially a means of connection (*Fig. 21*). They form new lines of communication, general ones between districts (east, west, north, south), specific ones between certain old or new key points such as railway stations or market places. Old streets were widened in order to accelerate traffic flow (rues Grenaté, La Reynie); blocked arteries were duplicated (rue Saint-Denis); and diagonals were cut (boulevard de Magenta, rue Turbigo). This overall network of arterial connections constituted what Haussmann described as a kind of "general circulatory system," which he subdivided into hierarchized tributary systems, each organized around a plaza, which is no longer a place in it itself but a traffic node, or what the Perfect termed *nodes of relation*. The enclosed plaza of the old order, a haven sheltered from traffic, has been suppressed.

Haussmann's own description of his plan is breathtaking. He intends "to cut a cross, north to south and east to west, through the center of Paris, bringing the city's cardinal points into direct communication."[26] The two axes, rue de Rivoli and boulevard Sébastapol with its extension boulevard Saint-Michel, will be completed by the double ring of outer boulevards (which include the continuation of those built under Louis XIV and a second ring), in order to provide a connecting framework within which will be incorporated the "system of the Etoile," the "system of the République," the "system of the Barrière d'Enfer," and so on.[27] The same circulatory scheme will be applied for the new districts to the west, on the undeveloped sites of the old suburban villages of Auteuil or Passy.

The originality of Haussmann's conception can be gauged by the degree of opposition he encountered—both from the Emperor and from the Chamber of Deputies—and by the difficulties he met with at the time of the 1858 Treaty when he attempted to impose his logic of comprehensive planning.

The second important idea behind Haussmann's planning was sanitation through the creation of voids—that is, through systematic recourse to a kind of surgery which has since been considered vandalism. Never before, for sure, had such wide-scale demolition been carried out, never at least in terms of solids and voids. With Haussmann, the notion of open space (*Freiflach*), still current today, came into being—open spaces which are not laid out for visual or ceremonial effect as in the Baroque, but simply for the negative reason that they are not to be filled in. And related to this idea of open spaces was that of verdured space which is very different from the old public garden in that it has lost its semiotic richness.

Demolition was badly needed, however. Today we find it

difficult to imagine the cramped, unsanitary conditions existing behind facades which, due to the newly born sense of history, the contemporary bourgeoisie had begun to find to be picturesque. Also, we have forgotten the vast number of structures which had progressively invaded all the city's open areas; some had even crept into the courtyard of the Louvre. Haussmann undeniably caused devastation, though nothing to compare with that wrought by the French Revolution. For since that time the archaeological vision had been born, and it forced the Prefect to spare monuments of the past.[28] But in the 1850's and 1860's, the idea of preserving an urban texture had not yet matured: Haussmann's most serious error was to destroy irrevocably the tightly woven and diversified fabric of the Île de la Cité, whose new blocks of giant buildings condemned it to death (*Fig. 19*).

Nonetheless, Haussmann's surgery had its positive side. Within the network of streets designed for traffic flow, he created a hierarchy of planted areas, which he divided into four categories: promenades like the Champs-Elysées; squares, the model of which Napoleon III had brought back from London; public gardens laid out in a romantic pattern (the most successful of these are the Montsouris and Buttes-Chaumont parks [*Fig. 24*]); and lastly, suburban parks situated at the eastern and western limits of Paris. In the latter, formerly royal forests, right-angled paths and star circles intended for the royal hunts in the seventeenth century were replaced by curved roads encircling artificial lakes.

In his *Mémoires*, Haussmann constantly brings up esthetic matters. But this aspect of his work is not original and can be summed up as a monotonous repetition of the principles of Neoclassicism: uniform frontage lines along broad, straight streets, research into perspective effects and location of monuments on a perspective axis. For Haussmann, esthetics are actually secondary, coming as a belated attempt to embellish streets which he had not originally laid out for reasons of beauty. Although indifferent in this respect, his work did not fail to impress some of his contemporaries as evidenced by Vienna and Berlin. But the real basis as well as the originality of his planning lies in the dual concept of a circulatory and respiratory system. This schema of regularization emerges during the last third of the nineteenth century as the fundamental verity of the capitalist-industrialist order. It will be referred to as the *Haussmann pattern* though it sometimes developed empirically outside the sphere of Parisian influence. For Paris offers the most systematic example of its application and served as a model for the majority of the other cities.

OTHER EXAMPLES

It is in Europe that the Haussmann process was most widely applied and in France that the Prefect's theories were carried to their ultimate consequences by the visionary Henry-Jules Borie (*Fig. 25*) and especially Eugène Hénard (1849–1923). Borie was a great admirer of Haussmann; he was an engineer who, in 1865, published an essay entitled "Aérodomes: essai sur un nouveau mode d'habitations applicable aux quartiers le plus mouvementés des grandes villes." His proposition was meant to improve daily life in the great demographic centers, among which he included London, Liverpool, Manchester, New York, Boston, and Chicago. He wished not only to keep these big cities, but also to increase their density; this was made possible through an improved multilevel system of circulation which:

1) occupied 73 percent of the city surface instead of 18 percent in Haussmann's Paris.

2) offered to pedestrians large streets on interrelated terraces 20 to 30 meters high; the schools were located on the upper terrace (the roof of the aérodome). "Moving rooms" (steam-powered elevators) enabled the people to climb from the lower-level streets to the upper-level ones. At all the levels the streets were interconnected by bridges and glassed-in galleries.

Hénard had a greater influence. As a theoretician we owe to him the invention of the rotary intersection, which regularizes traffic flow around plazas (*Fig. 26*), as well as an analysis of the different categories of movement which is more detailed than Le Corbusier's; its logical conclusion is the creation of an elevated ground level and the importance given to underground transportation. In the projects he conceived for Paris, his radical approach led him to suppress any cultural obstacles which might stand in the way of widening and straightening streets. Thus, rue de Richelieu was to be made as wide as the Champs-Elysées and was to be cut by a new perpendicular throughway which would also cut through the Palais Royal. Hénard's conception of the city as projected in his drawings (*Fig. 27*) is not without resemblance to later sketches by Le Corbusier. Practically speaking, his only achievement in Paris was the Alexander III perspective, which he created for the 1900 World's Fair.

In Germany, especially after the war of 1870, the Haussmann layout, with the architect Joseph Stübben (1845–1936) as a major exponent, frequently inspired total (Berlin, Cologne [*Fig. 28*]) or partial (Dresden, Munich) restructuration. However, increasing emphasis on archaeological and historical studies, and, to a larger extent, survival well into the nineteenth century of medieval traditions in old towns that often passed without transition into an industrial phase, resulted in the elaboration of circulatory and respiratory systems with a greater respect for the creations of the past. Old elements such as city gates or sections of walls were systematically incorporated into new, significant complexes; and—more important—old and new town were subtly interrelated. This is particularly evident in the treatment of the single and double ring boulevards designed in the place of ancient ramparts (*Fig. 29*). In addition the function of housing is more carefully studied than in France, and is often set up in parallels and incorporated into networks of side streets that are removed from the main traffic arteries.

In Spain a major problem of regularization arose in Barcelona. Antonio Rovira y Trias (1816–1889), winner of a competition organized in 1859 by the city government of Barcelona, proposed to solve the problem by creating a system of radiating boulevards in trapezoidal sectors between the old town and its extension (*Fig. 30*). The engineer Ildefonso Cerdá (1816–1876) was chosen instead to carry out his own plan for the city's extension (*Fig. 31*) but a satisfactory traffic system serving both Cerdá's scheme of a gigantic checkerboard and the old town was not worked out for a number of years. Eventually the traffic situation was partially remedied by creation of the Rondas (anticipated Cerdá's plan) and the plaza de Cataluña (somewhat smaller than the gigantic square proposed in Rovira's plan) at the top of the old town (*Fig. 32*).

Throughout Europe we also find other fragmentary efforts: the regularization of certain quarters (such as in Antwerp [*Fig. 33*], Brussels, or Dresden [*Fig. 34*]) or simply the unsystematic opening of main arteries like those in the Viviani Plan for Rome, namely the two axes, Corso Vittorio Emanuele (from the Tiber to Piazza Venezia) and Via Nazionale (*Fig. 35*). In London, similar efforts were the work of official organizations such as the Office of Woods and Forests, the Metropolitan Board of Works, and later the London County Council, who for expediency's sake cut wide empirical openings through the old urban fabric: Trafalgar Square, New Oxford Street, Shaftesbury Avenue, Charing Cross Road, Kingsway.

In the United States the Haussmann pattern made a belated appearance, for urban disorder had come there late, produced by the juxtaposition of several independent checkerboard layouts (as in San Francisco or Chicago) or by the inadequacy of the checkerboard as a circulatory system beyond a certain degree of expansion (*Figs. 36–37*). Thus in 1909, the plan devised for Chicago by Daniel Burnham (1846–1912) and Edward Bennett

(1874?–1954)—the first major comprehensive project for regularizing an American city—results primarily from the desire to create a traffic system which would solve the problems from the city's division into independent gridiron sections (*Fig. 38*). In the initial scheme, which was only partially executed, a wide central esplanade (N.-S.) was planned, which would serve as the starting point for ten radial streets. These included the new wide central axis (Empress Street) running perpendicular to Lake Michigan, and six diagonal streets; three wide circumvallating avenues completed this basic arterial structure. A highly elaborated respiratory system was designed to incorporate three large parks—Lincoln Park to the north, Grant Park in the center, and Jackson Park to the south—interconnected by a continuous strip of greenery which provided a structural frame for the grafting on of secondary parks. We shall briefly review the origin of this complex type of urban lung known as the Park System.

THE URBAN PARK FROM PAXTON TO OLMSTED

Parallel with comprehensive regularization a partial regularization process—or what can be considered an element of regularization, the city park—has been developed in the open cities of the Anglo-Saxon countries. Haussmann had borrowed the idea from Great Britain, but he reduced it almost entirely to its respiratory function. For this reason, it is important to discuss the semantically richer prototype which had served as the model for the Buttes-Chaumont (*Fig. 24*) or Parc Montsouris in France and was later given new improvements elsewhere.

With the growth of the city in nineteenth-century England, city parks belonging to royal or seignorial domains were preserved by far-sighted landowners, with the same concern as the squares which give increased value to the developments. At the same time, however, due to the growth of an urban proletariat, new districts were spreading on the periphery, in which the *back-to-back* pattern of residential construction resulted in a total absence of greenery. At this point Edwin Chadwick (1800–1890) and special research committees advanced their theories concerning "The Effect of Public Walks and Gardens on the Health and Morals of the Lower Classes" and called for regularization of the suburbs and the development of a new urban element, a new type of park, designed not only for the purpose of ventilation but also for the recreation and relaxation of the masses.

The prototype for this appeared at Birkenhead, a suburb of Liverpool, where in 1814 Joseph Paxton was called by the municipal government to design and build what became the prototype of the new city park (*Fig. 39*). The celebrated gardener decided to surround it with houses, and in draining the terrain he excavated sufficient earth to enclose a couple of artificial ponds of irregular form. In the tradition of Lancelot Brown,[29] he contrasted leafy and wooded border areas with central lawns and he counterbalanced those areas of the park reserved for walks with the open spaces created for sports and games. Not until much later were the latter introduced into continental parks, which for the time being remained gardens. But the most interesting aspect of the Birkenhead Park was its circulatory system consisting of two completely independent networks: an irregular one of narrow pedestrian paths and a roadway for carriages and horses, that ran all along the outer edge of the park and divided it across the waist.

In the United States the idea of a recreation field integrated into the urban fabric was picked up and expanded by Frederick Law Olmsted (1822–1903), who wrote, following his first trip to England: " I was ready to admit that in democratic America there was nothing to be thought of as comparable with this people's garden."[30] With Olmsted, the urban park will be more thoroughly integrated into the city (which in this case is a metropolis), and at the same time more completely contrasted with it, both as a place of recreation and as a *segment of unspoiled nature*.

In 1856, Olmsted is requested by Calvert Vaux (1824–1895) to take part with him in a competition organized by the city of New York for the creation of an urban park. Their project is the winner. In 1857 Olmsted is appointed Park Superintendent. Central Park (*Fig. 40*) becomes the new prototype succeeding Birkenhead.

From the outset, Olmsted adopts, Haussmann-style, a prospective vision. He designs the park, which was still then suburban, for the time when it would be at the center of Manhattan's steadily developing checkerboard and hemmed in on all sides by buildings.[31] It had to act as the lungs of the city without becoming an impediment to communication. The conception of Central Park's circulatory network is a major contribution to a theory especially favored during the second half of the nineteenth century: the separation of traffic systems. For the first time in history, four traffic networks (for pedestrians, riders, fast and slow vehicles) were planned to function simultaneously, yet independently. Going a step further, Olmsted brought the third dimension into play, making use of tunnels, viaducts and any irregularities in the terrain in order to carry out his system.

Olmsted did not lay the park out in the European tradition. Rather than reshape and domesticate nature, he deliberately designed it in an unspoiled, almost primitive state.[32] His purpose was to let it be itself in contrast with the urban fabric. Through this stark opposition, the city becomes more a city and nature, more nature. Thus, in the case of Manhattan, where man had suppressed the character of the landscape in his effort to achieve a regular checkerboard of asphalt and stone, Olmsted chose to preserve accidents of terrain and the irregular character of the area's original topography. On this point he was explicit. His aim was to "secure an antithesis of objects of vision to those of the streets"; not satisfied with avoiding the inconveniences of the city, he wanted to create "an opposite class of conditions."[33] Olmsted, in fact, set apart a kind of reservation, which he endeavored to shield from the vision of the future *wall of China* that would rise around it and to avoid the various constructions that Reptonian tradition assigned specifically to parks. Even the gardening technique used in planting was to be based on the principles of opposition and contrast.

Thus the park as conceived by Olmsted appears semantically rich. Its relation with the urban totality became more complex as the American cities requested Olmsted's services. He had already ascribed a regional function to Central Park, but from 1870 on he developed his idea of the Park System: a network of urban parks systematically laid out and interconnected by stretches of greenery. His first application of this scheme was in Boston, in 1891. He was, in fact, the creator of an element of regularization which up to 1857 had been practically nonexistent, but by 1902, on the eve of his death, had been adopted by 796 American towns.[34]

PAXTON'S GREAT VICTORIAN WAY AND THE LONDON UNDERGROUND RAILWAY

Until the twentieth century the Landed Estate remained the basic unit of city planning in Great Britain. However, one project was elaborated which, although it was never executed, came about in the same spirit as Haussmann's. This was a study made by Joseph Paxton (1803–1865) in 1855, at that time a member of Parliament, in answer to a report prepared by the Select Committee on Metropolitan Improvement. Its object was the improvement of the *general system* of communications (*Fig. 41*).

Paxton's approach to the problem involves exactly the same clinical procedure as Haussmann's. He thinks in comprehensive terms, considers the city as a whole. He viewed it in its historical perspective, criticized former plans, analyzed the various forms and currents of traffic flow and inventoried existing streets.

Paxton's solution achieved the same results as Haussmann albeit using entirely different means. He proposed connecting all of London's railway stations by means of a transportation belt whose main axis was oriented east-west (the predominant

24

direction of traffic flow). Designed to avoid duplication of any large existing streets, and to preserve any real estate worth saving, the belt was an unbroken stretch of ten miles and a furlong; it was completed north of the Thames by a one-mile two-furlong branch road running north-south through the Waterloo Road district and behind Piccadilly Circus.

Paxton's great thoroughfare, later called the "Great Victorian Way," was devised to reduce to fifteen minutes the maximum time required for travel between any two points on its perimeter. It was projected as a glassed-in arcade, 22 meters wide, 33 meters high, and flanked on either side by railway tracks in several layers, beginning at the height of 7½ to 8 meters. Thus fast transit was assured by a system of eight lines, both express and local, while on ground level the arcade was an asphalt street protected from bad weather, noise, and dust, and heated along certain sections in winter. Between the City and Regent Street it was lined with shops; during the day it was restricted to the circulation of pedestrians and private vehicles, but could be used at night for transportation of merchandise.

Though Paxton's project was worked out in detail from the point of view of construction and finance, and was supported in Parliament, it remained on paper. George F. Chadwick (see Bibliography) has, however, accurately pointed out its value as a visionary conception and the significance of its three-dimensional arrangement of traffic. As far as his affinity with Haussmann, it should be noted that Paxton took the rapidity of mechanical transportation into account in a systematic way.

The spirit of the Great Victorian Way to some extent found expression in the plan for the London Underground, whose first section was opened in 1863. Actually the underground with its fast, direct, and interconnected lines constitutes a London counterpart of the Haussmann system, a concretization of the same process. Its construction was contemporaneous with the *grands travaux de Paris*, and inversely, the question arises whether it is not the extensive elaboration of a ground level traffic system in Paris that delayed construction of its Metro until 1900.

COMMENTARIES AND METALANGUAGE

Urbanists in charge of regularization not only drafted projects but also discussed them in an abundant literature that included their comments and theories. The nineteenth century is the century of criticism: in the case of city planning, there is a definite correlation between the semantic impoverishment of the urban system itself, and the appearance of theoretical treatises preceding and justifying various practical proposals. It is in these texts that one can directly appraise the mutation by which city planning acquired a critical dimension. Haussmann's principles and his *Mémoires* (a justification by hindsight, which in fact returns to the a-priori arguments of his *decrees* and speeches as Prefect) are echoed both by Paxton's testimony, *The Evidence*,[35] and by the didactic writings of German architects like Stübben. But the most astonishing written work we unquestionably owe to Cerdá.

In the first volume (eight hundred pages) of the *Teoría General de Urbanización* (1867),[36] written at the same time as the *Mémoires* and twenty-three years before Stübben's *Der Städtebau*, all the themes of the new literature are collected, related, and set forth in detail: namely, historical perspective as applied to urban history; research into a taxonomy of not only cities and planning methods but also of urban elements (traffic arteries, streets and plazas, housing, gardens and so on), which must be based on historical evolution as well as functional analysis; a priority of traffic problems in any planning for the present or future.

In Cerdá's work, this semantic priority given to urban circulation is symbolized by the fact that this function is the basis of his classification of cities, the criterion by which the various phases of urban history are put in chronological order: The structure of the most ancient cities is adapted to pedestrian circulation (*locomoción pedestre*); later it is transformed to fit, successively, horseback (*locomoción ecuestre*), an intermediate stage of dragged sledges (*rastrera*), and finally the wheeled vehicle (*rodada*). The latter is in turn divided into ordinary (horse power) and perfected (*perfeccionada*), which used the steam engine and had just been worked out in Cerdá's time.[37] A distinction is thus made between the traditional and the improved *rodada* which is contemporary with *ciencia urbanizadora* (urban science). One must also notice the importance given by the Spanish engineer to the philology upon which he grounds his theories. Through etymological analysis he was better able to penetrate the meaning of terms that are traditionally employed to designate what is urban, and further to justify the invention of a new expression—*una palabra nueva*—for use in the new planning. The language of planning, which came out of critical analysis, is a scientific language, destined by its very nature to become the attribute of a planning *establishment*—in other words, a metalanguage[38]—though Cerdá himself never claimed this and no doubt was unaware of it.

If we analyze the actual accomplishments of regularization as well as its projects and metalanguages, we may define the process as follows:

1) The city is conceived as an object: Both theoretically and in its reality, the modern city came out of the same type of reflective effort that produced the nineteenth-century concepts of art and labor. The city-exhibitions first held in Germany at the beginning of the twentieth century were the symbol of this reification—literally an incarnation of nineteenth-century theory.

As a consequence of this process and of the century's general awareness of history, the concepts of historical monument and preservation of the past were created. The nineteenth century is the first to be concerned with the conservation of the past as a whole. The leader in this respect was France (in 1837 the *Commission des Monuments Historiques* was created),[39] but her measures of conservation were directed at isolated edifices and not at urban ensembles.

2) An analytical method is used, both in the study of the object and in the elaboration of projects. The key words are *classification* and *system*.

Its use of classification, in which visual factors were extremely important, appears to have been borrowed from the natural sciences. Moreover, the concept of function evolved by the new biology becomes the basis of the systems created by the city planners who also apply to the city biological images like circulation, nucleus, and cell.

3) Two objectives are given exclusive priority: traffic and hygiene.

PSEUDURBIAS AND REDUCED BEHAVIOR

While the big city of the industrial era became a pole of attraction and fascination, it also began, as early as the 1850's, to provoke reactions of escape (*Fig. 42*). While it inspired regularization on the one hand, on the other it gave rise to the creation outside city limits of new agglomerations which were reduced in size and function and which corresponded to a new value in industrial society: housing. Two different and representative types of accretions occurred: 1) residential communities designed for wealthy or middle-class residents and 2) workers' colonies (or villages or towns). All of them we shall call *pseudurbias*. They were an outgrowth of hybrid planning which, though crucial, was nonetheless of a retrogressive tendency and indicated a reduced pattern of behavior with respect to the rich and diversified vocation of the city.

RESIDENTIAL TOWNS AND VILLAGES IN THE SUBURBS

As members of the upper middle class began fleeing the evils of the city to live in the country, there developed simultaneously the concept of the country, as a sort of negative counterpart to the concept of the city. Thus in 1858, Alphonse Pallu decided to create Le Vésinet (*Fig. 43*), a precocious model of the residential town on a 436-hectare site on the road from Paris to Saint-Germain.

This community represented a haven of domestic life from which various forms of trade and industry had been banned. The only civic elements and public utilities allowed were those considered essential to residential *constructions and needs*—railway station, post office, schools, church, shops for vital commodities —which were grouped together away from private houses. Enjoyment of a picturesque countryside was the key attraction, in view of which the landscape gardeners Olive and Count de Choulot created a river and five lakes and dispersed the houses in an area designed in the English fashion with a public park as its center.

In Great Britain, the same residential and rural objectives inspired Richard Norman Shaw (1831–1912) when, between 1875 and 1881, at the request of Jonathan Carr, he built the suburban village of Bedford Park, at Turnham Green (*Fig. 44*). Church, cooperative store, club, and inn were the basic public faculties of this *artistic* agglomeration, which in this case was designed for a less wealthy section of the population. Landscaping was considered less important than the development of prototypes in housing. Detached or semidetached villas were designed of brick in the Dutch style by this master of English domestic architecture, whose main concern was the interior layout of his homes.

In this type of community, typical in Great Britain, the Germanic countries, and Belgium, the esthetic aspect did not really mature until the end of the century. Its supreme achievement was Hampstead Garden Suburb (1907; *Fig. 45*), designed by Parker and Unwin. Here analysis of the disposition of houses and paths discloses a series of precise intentions: to create a counterpart of countryside offering varied views and picturesqueness; to secure an intimate space, to ensure privacy for the dwellings, isolated not only from each other but from traffic and from whatever might recall the noises of the city.[40]

28

WORKERS' TOWNS, COLONIES, AND VILLAGES

Certain employers decided to leave the city in order to provide healthier and especially more productive living conditions for their workers. At the edge of the big cities or in the open country, where land was less expensive, more space could be allotted to each individual and dwellings could be better designed and constructed.

In the early phase, these new working-class agglomerations followed a very rudimentary pattern, revealing no concern with matters of esthetics. They were characterized by separation of housing and working functions, orthogonal layouts, and standardization of elements. A basic minimum of public utilities and services was provided (the *nefarious* pub was more often than not excluded by moralizing employers), while the public park represented the only element of luxury. All the effort went into housing, whose models became one of the attractions of the first world's fairs. The movement was inaugurated by Great Britain, and was followed by industrialized Europe, and then by the United States. The varying characteristics of these settlements reflect different degrees of a benevolent paternalism on the part of employers who might or might not choose to welcome residents who were not connected with their business.

Bessbrook (Ireland), created in 1846 by the Benjamin Ward Richardson family for their 2,500 workers, boasted a library, one hotel, and two squares. The famous Saltaire, founded in 1852 by Titus Salt for the 4,000 workers in his textile mill outside Bradford, was more austere, with a park affording its only greenery. In France, the movement was led by the textile manufacturers of Alsace. The Mulhouse *Société des cités ouvrières* was founded in 1853; its only achievement was the creation of regular groups of small houses placed back-to-back or in blocks of four, with front court and back garden (*Fig. 46*). In Germany, Krupp's first settlements, dating from 1870, were not any more original and did not even enjoy private gardens. In the United States, the plan for Pullman City (near Chicago) (*Fig. 47*), where the industrialist George M. Pullman relocated his plant in 1867, was equally unelaborate, although elements of greater commodity were provided. Houses were equipped with running water and sewage disposal. The town had a commercial and cultural center in the Arcade, an isolated building of 80 by 54 meters and 26 meters high, which had a covered gallery running through its middle. There one could find savings banks, meeting halls, a library, and a theater designed to seat 1,000, but no public bar.

In the 1880's the development of the industrial settlement

entered a second phase, generally localized in Great Britain and Germany. It is characterized by plans that did not incorporate new functions but new values, namely esthetic principles and individualism, in the development of which parks and greenery are to play an important role. The notion of the model house is succeeded by that of the model village.

The pioneers in this field were the English manufacturers. As early as 1879, the Cadbury family purchased 183 hectares of land five miles from Birmingham, where they built Bournville (*Fig. 48*) for the workers in their chocolate factories. Not only were the cottage types designed with great variety, but the picturesque is the explicit aim of the overall plan; the curve was predominant in the layout of streets, which were all planted with a carefully selected variety of trees, and gardens were to form by statute an inviolable part of the whole. Port Sunlight (*Fig. 49*), a settlement begun in 1888 by the Lever family, was more compact but boasted a central park as well as two traffic systems—a circuit of tree-lined streets 12.2 to 21.3 meters wide for vehicles and a circuit of paths for pedestrians—which had been designed to ensure peace and quiet and to be visually pleasing.

In Germany, an analysis of the progressive development of the Krupp workers' settlements reveals the gradual triumph of romantic esthetics. Typical of the first phase, in 1872, was Schederhof (*Fig. 50*), with identical houses, a rectangular road pattern, and an English style public park placed at the edge of the town. The transformation began in 1894 with Alfredshof 1 (*Fig. 51*), where an attempt was made to create picturesque (pseudo-medieval) architectural effects. At Atenhof 1 (*Fig. 52*) and Alfredshof 2 (*Fig. 53*) (which was an extension to the north of Alfredshof 1), however, the overall plan itself becomes pic-torial as it breaks into pieces, loses the former regularity, and re-incorporates continuous stretches of houses. A little later, Margarethenhof was designed in the image of the old German village, and Altenhof 2 broke completely with the straight line and building alignment, skillfully alternating high and low tempo and provided with two networks, one for vehicles, another for pedestrians.

Possibly the most striking example of the picturesque was Agneta Park (*Fig. 54*), built in 1883 in Holland by the industrialist Van Marken. Here the public elements (schools, bakery, co-operative store) were dispersed at the four corners of the com-munity whose center was a lake.

Analysis brings out, in spite of obvious differences in their content, the structural identity of residential town and workers' settlement in the second half of the nineteenth century. Their planning, elementary though it may seem, has been discussed here primarily because it represented the beginning of a process of reduction (possibly arbitrary) whose development has continued during the twentieth century. Also, once defined, pseudurbias can more easily be differentiated from garden cities, with which they have been compared and associated too frequently.[41]

PRE-URBANISM AND URBANISM: THE PROGRESSIST MODEL

In the process of regularization, urban "disorder" was examined in an effort to extract a potential order out of it; this order itself was not questioned, however. The term *urbanism* will be used to describe the process that radically contested this hidden order and ultimately led to the a-priori construction of a new and *different* one.

Though urbanism in this sense was not actually practiced before the end of the nineteenth century, it was preceded by a purely theoretical form of planning that anticipated it. Speculation of this kind was engaged in by a group of social and political thinkers who aspired to the complete restructuring of society—in which the city was but one element. Their cities were utopias.

Nonetheless, we may designate them as examples of *pre-urbanism*,[42] since in creating imaginary constructions like Phalange, Hygeia, Icara, or Nowhere, they produced the two basic models of spatial organization later to be retained by urbanism. One of these models, looking to the future and inspired by a vision of social progress, we shall call *progressist*. The other, nostalgic in outlook, is inspired by the vision of a cultural community and may therefore be called *culturalist*.

Analysis of both these models, in their original purity and their ideological context of pre-urbanism, is essential to any understanding of urbanism, whose underlying motives have since been obscured by history's unpredictable twists and turns.

THE PROGRESSIST MODEL—PRE-URBANISM

The progressist model of planning was the first to emerge and is also the most important because out of it came what is today considered to be modern urban space. Although hygienists like Sir Benjamin Ward Richardson (1828–1896) contributed to its elaboration, this model of planning owed itself primarily to founders of socialism, namely Robert Owen (1771–1858), Charles Fourier (1772–1837), and Etienne Cabet (1788–1856), who while condemning the power of industrial society to alienate, yet saw in it the most effective means of liberation, provided that the machine could be used to transform man and his world.

However, among the socialists who denounced the blight and squalor of the industrial city, Marx and Engels never proposed any replacement model. They considered it an illusion to plan the city of the future before the conditions required for its realization, namely revolution and its related restructuring, had been fulfilled. Not until the power was in the hands of the proletariat could a new world be built. This attitude, which persisted in various currents of European socialist thought during the second half of the nineteenth century, was later expressed by Lenin and his disciples, at the time of the October Revolution, as can be seen in the *ABC of Communism* by Bukharin and Preobraschensky.

The other progressists, however, and notably those whom Marx called the Utopian Socialists, were to express their faith and their will to transform society in the form of imaginary cities which, though different, possessed a common spatial structure. Inasmuch as a detailed description of each vision would be too lengthy, we shall focus our analysis on the characteristics of the common model they share.

The progressist concept of space breaks with the old contiguous order of things, which regularization had not rejected but had simply modified by cutting into it. From the outset, the progressist spatial pattern is not based on continuity of solids but on a continuity of voids in which constructed elements have burst apart. Air, light, and greenery have become symbols of progress, and dispersal is considered essential to physical hygiene. Owen, for example, arranged the dwellings of his model towns, designed for 1,200 inhabitants, within square areas which are planted with gardens in the center and surrounded by 400 to 600 hectares of land (*Fig. 55*). These small communities dot the countryside like Fourier's *phalanstères* (*Fig. 58*) and the various versions of the built-up communautary idea (*Fig. 57*).

The relationship founded on contiguity which previously prevailed in the organization of urban systems is replaced by a relation founded on association; edifices are grouped in a discontinuous manner, according to function. Devised for reasons of efficiency and productivity, this functional classification is the origin of zoning. In all the plans of these authors housing is separated from recreation and work, the latter being further classified by type. Owen's squares are made up of dwellings grouped into what was actually a single building (*Fig. 56*), with mechanical and industrial activities located outside the unit, followed by agricultural functions. Fourier follows the same pattern with the wings of his Social Palace designed to house certain public utilities that Owen placed at the center of the

1. Hygeia, a model town to have been established on Romantic-Classical principles in Kentucky across the Ohio River from Cincinnati. The plan was drawn in England by the architect J. B. Papworth in 1827, but never came to fruition.

2. Berlin in the late eighteenth century, with its fortifications and extensions.

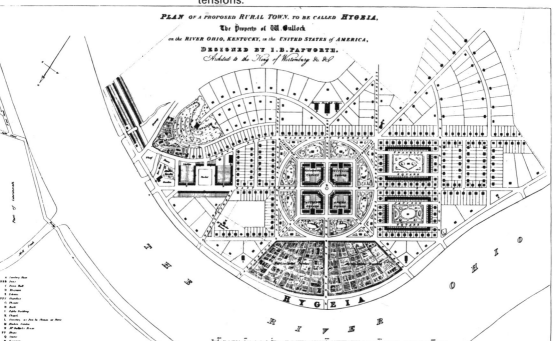

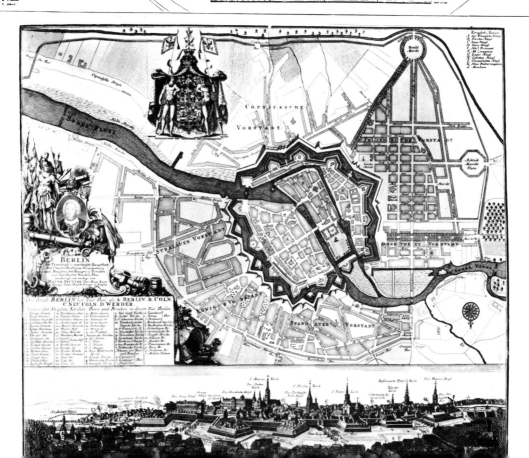

3. Bremen in the eighteenth century.

4. Bremen, c. 1890, The Ring promenade.

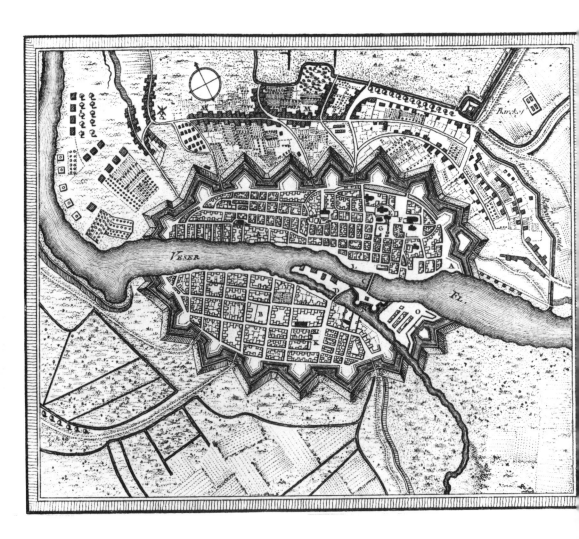

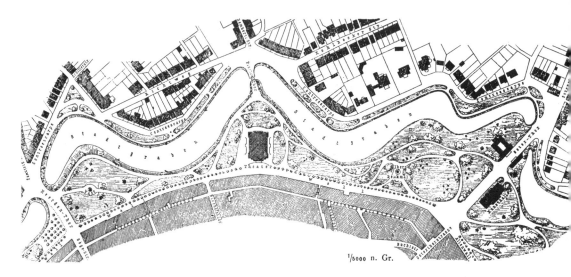

1/5000 n. Gr.

5. Vienna before the Ringstrasse development; view toward Karls-
kirche from the Augustiner bastion. Suburban development in the
distance.

6. Paris. 120° intersection of rue de Rivoli and rue de Castiglione, c.
1885.

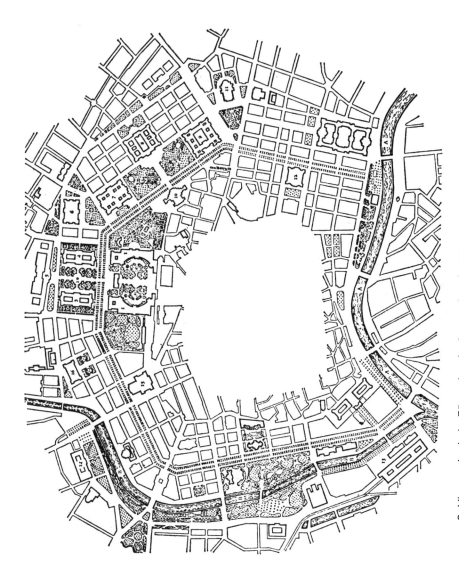

7. London. Regent Street, the Quadrant, 1822.

8. Vienna. Ludwig Förster's winning project for Ringstrasse, 1859.

9. London. Balloon view taken over Hampstead, 1851. 1- Portland
   Place; 2- Carlton House; 3- Mayfair; 4- Belgravia; 5- Regent's
   Park; 6- Covent Garden; 7- Regent Street.

10. Detail of balloon view of London.
   1- Covent Garden; 2- Bedford Square; 3- Tavistock Square;
   4- Gordon Square.

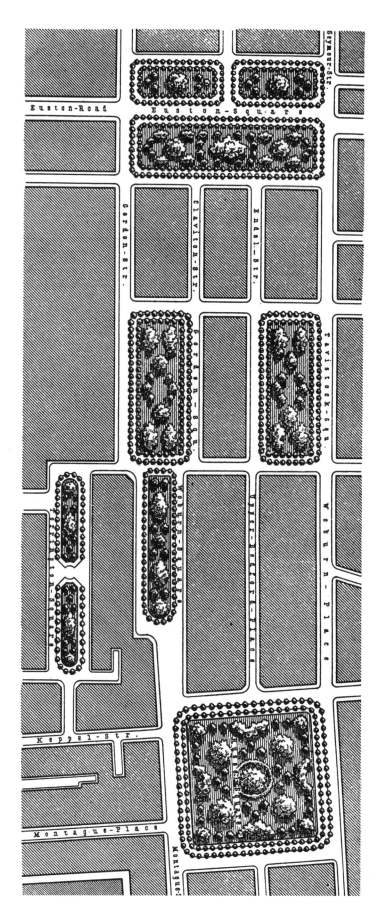

1. Squares in the West End of London, c. 1890.
   Top to bottom: Euston, Tavistock and Gordon, Woburn and Torring-
   ton, and Russell squares.

12. Plan of Figs Mead (1834; left, hatched) and Somers' Town (center).

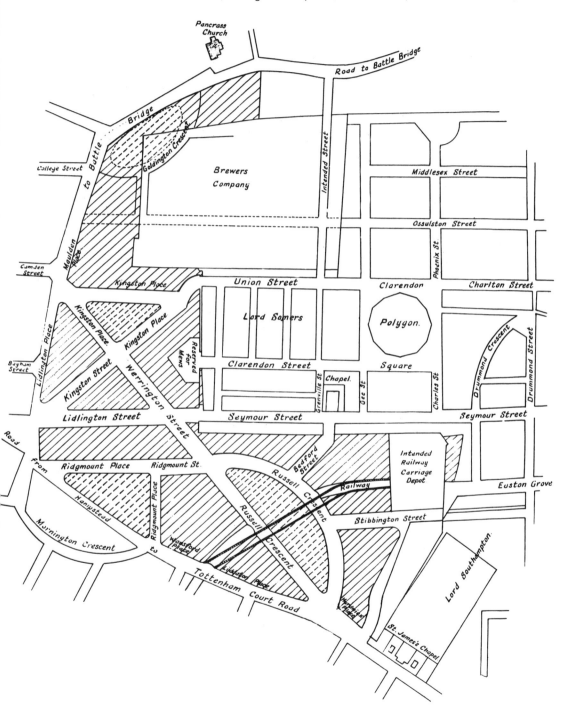

Pancras Church

Road to Battle Bridge

Bridge

College Street

Goldington Crescent

Maiden Place

to Battle

Brewers Company

Intended Street

Middlesex Street

Ossulston Street

Phoenix St.

Camden Street

Kingston Place

Union Street

Clarendon

Charlton Street

Lidlington Place

Kingston Place

Kingston Place

Kingston Place

Werrington Street

Kingston Street

Lord Somers

Reserved for Mews

Clarendon Street

Polygon.

Square

Drummond Crescent

Drummond Street

Bayham Street

Grenville St.

Chapel.

Gee St.

Charles St.

Lidlington Street

Ridgmount Place

Ridgmount St.

Seymour Street

Bedford Street

Russell Crescent

Seymour Street

Ridgmount Place

Intended Railway Carriage Depot

Euston Grove

Road from

Hampstead

Mornington Crescent

Woodsford Place

Lidlington Place

Russell Crescent

Railway

Stibbington Street

Lord Southampton

Tottenham Court Road

St. James's Chapel

13. Plan of Adelaide and North Adelaide, Australia, as drawn by P. F.
    Sinnett in 1881.

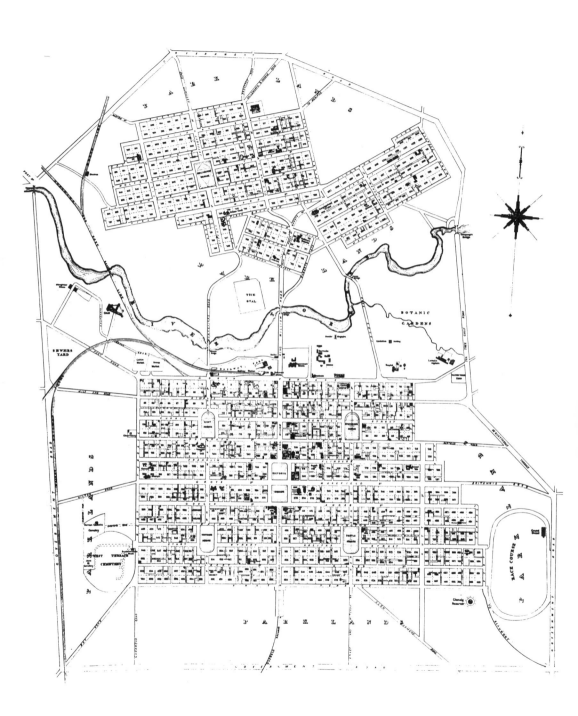

15. New York City. Plan of 1811. The locations of the proposed Washington Square (1), Union Square (2), and Madison Square (3) are indicated.

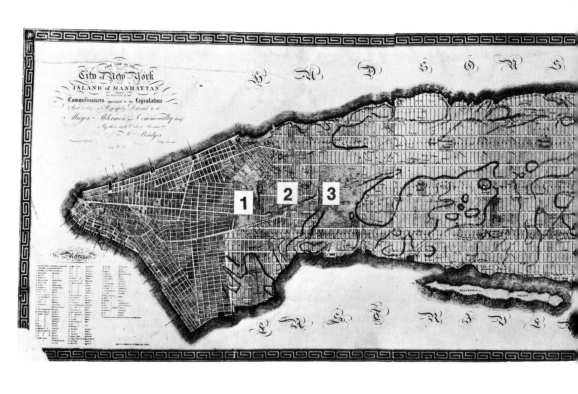

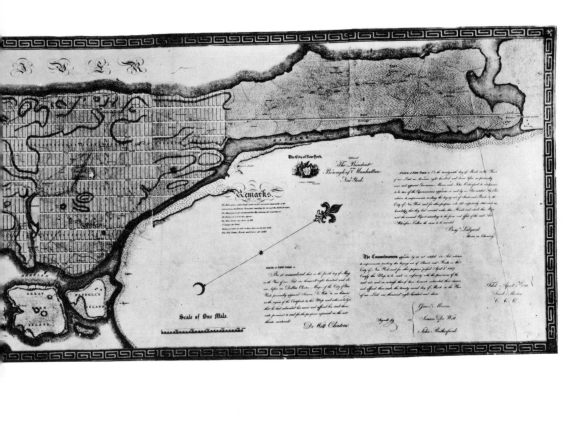

Scale of One Mile.

16. Paris. Demolition for the boulevard Saint-Michel, 1856.

17. Paris. Grading on the boulevard Malesherbes, July 6, 1864.

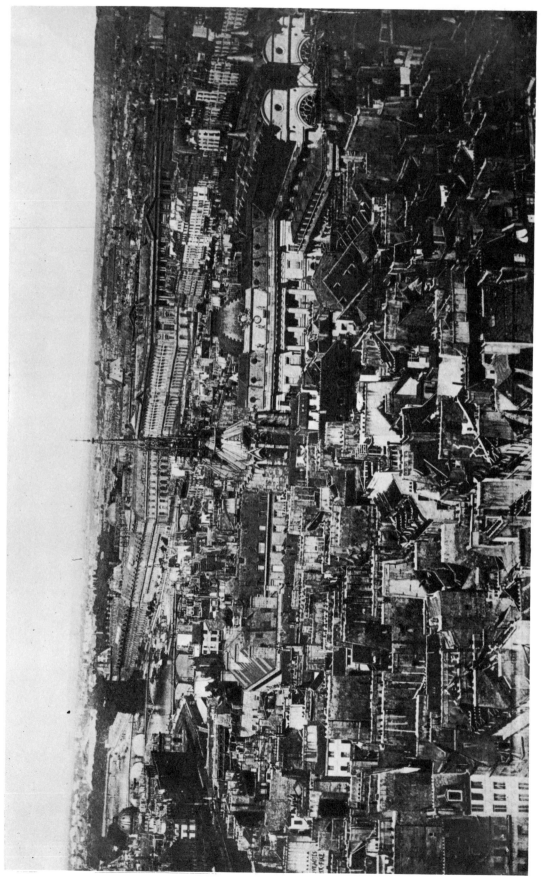

18. Paris. Central part of the Île de la Cité, 1854.

19. Paris. Panorama from the Tour Saint-Jacques, 1867.

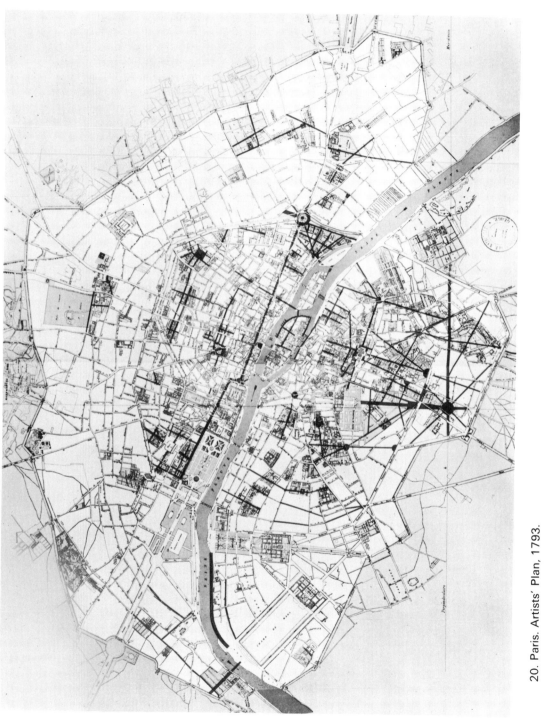

20. Paris. Artists' Plan, 1793.

21. Paris. Artists' Plan, detail showing
1- Saint Sulpice; 2- the Observatory; 3- the Val de Grâce.

22. Haussmann's projected transformation of Paris as presented by
Jean Alphand, c. 1867.

23. Detail of Plan of Paris made for Haussmann in 1866 (sheet 7). A
lower left is junction of boulevards Port-Royal and Saint-Michel
with boulevard Montparnasse off plan on left.

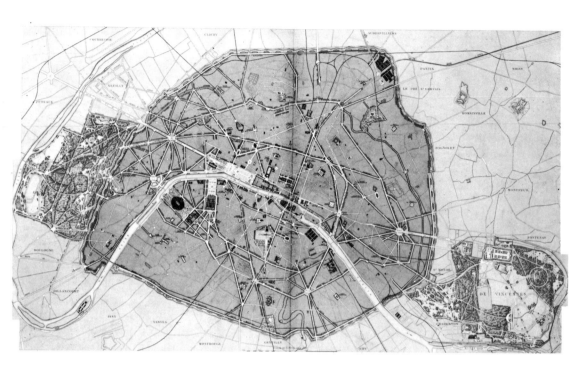

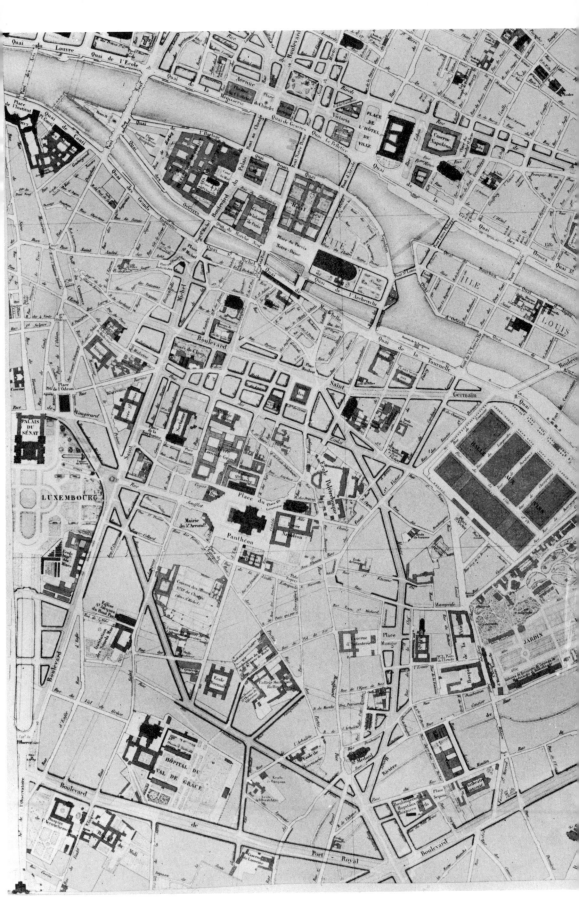

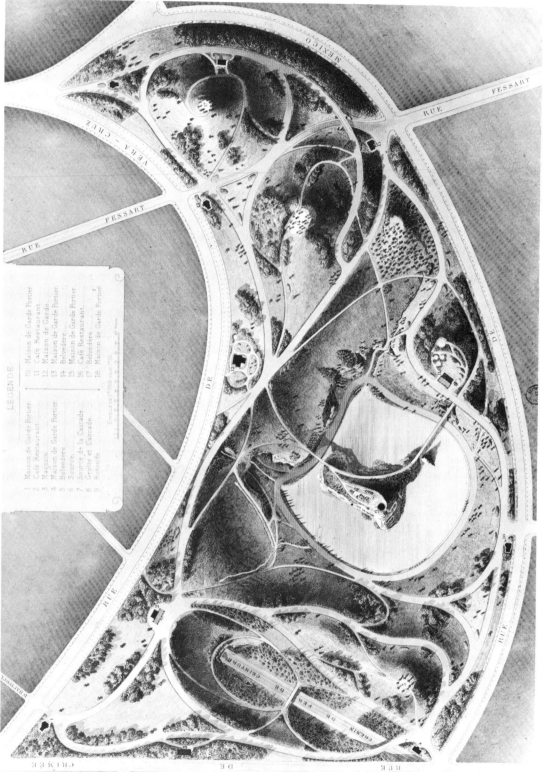

24. Paris. Plan of the park of Buttes-Chaumont, c. 1867.

25. Aérodomes, a project by the engineer Henry-Jules Borie, 1865.

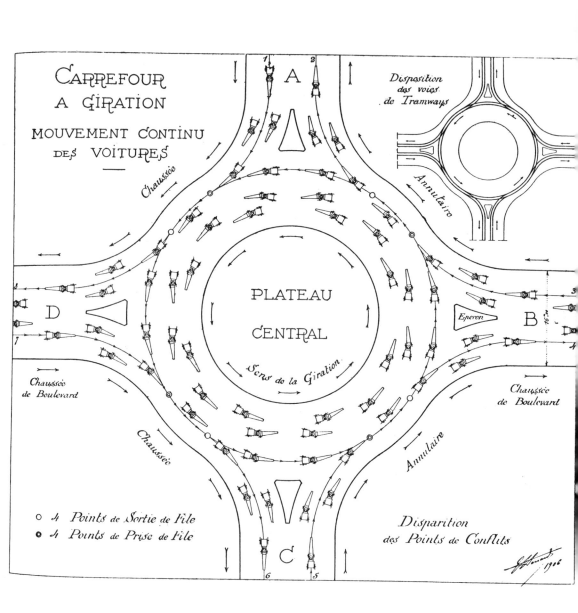

27. Hénard's project for a great cross-axis of an east-west transversal and a north-south avenue in Paris, 1904.
   A. Actual state of area north of the Louvre and the Tuileries Garden, showing rue de Rivoli at bottom (22 meters wide) and boulevard Sébastopol at right (30 meters wide).
   B. Hénard's suggestion for a 35-meter-wide avenue to bisect the avenue du Palais-Royal and the enlargement of the rue de Richelieu to 40 meters wide.

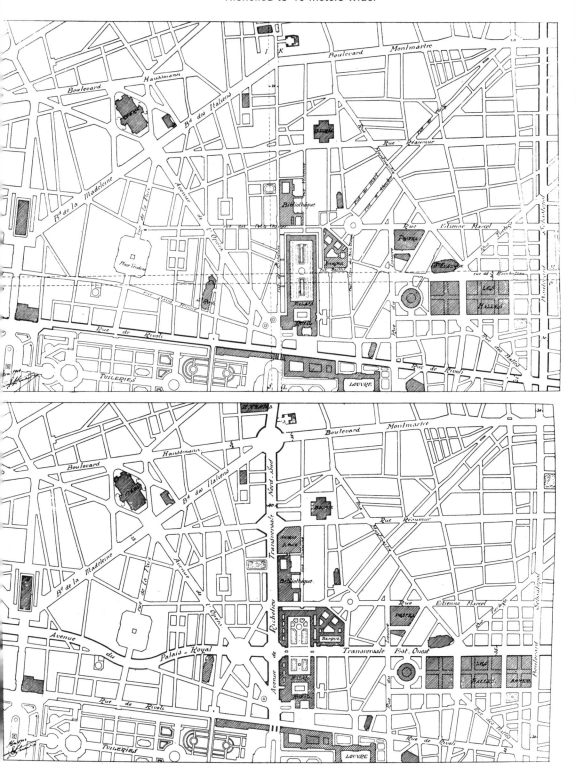

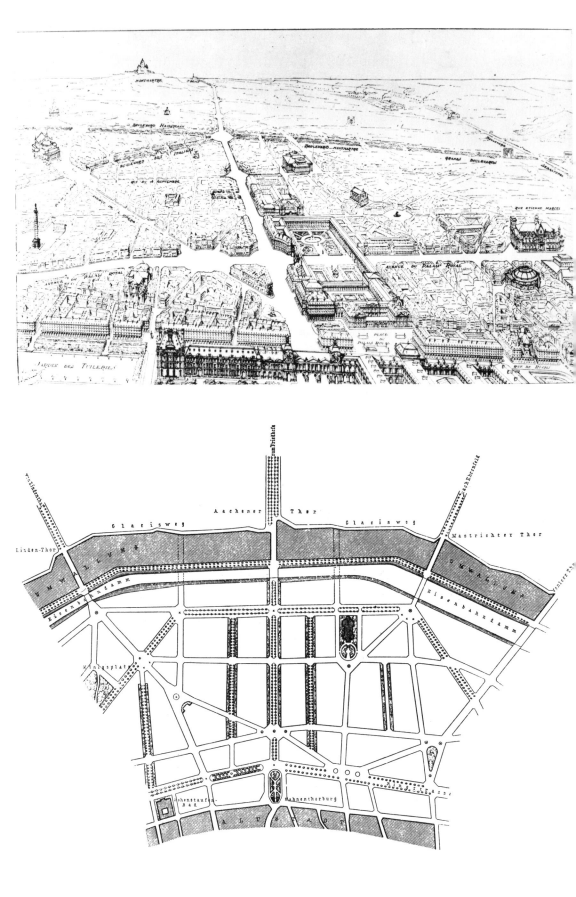

7 C. Bird's-eye view of Hénard's project.

8. Cologne. Detail of town plan, c. 1890.

29. Szeged, Hungary. Plan of the late nineteenth century, showing streets, buildings, and house numbers.

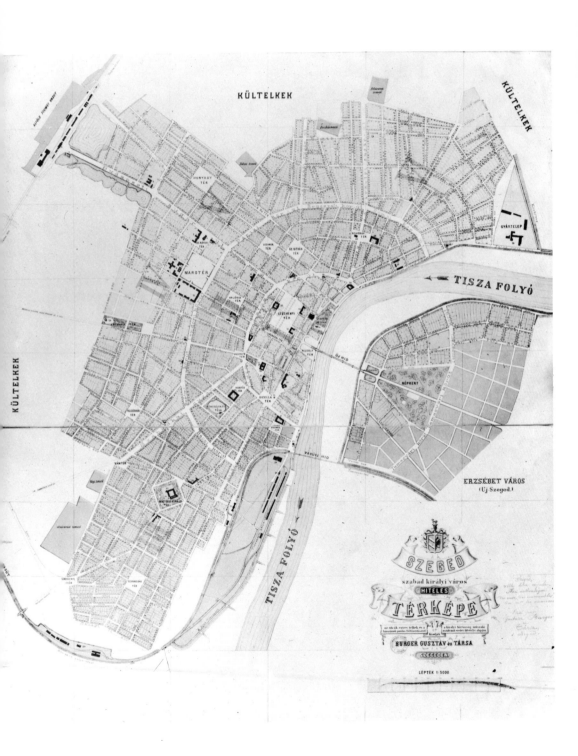

30. Plan for the expansion of Barcelona by Antonio Rovira y Trias, winner of the first prize in competition of 1859.

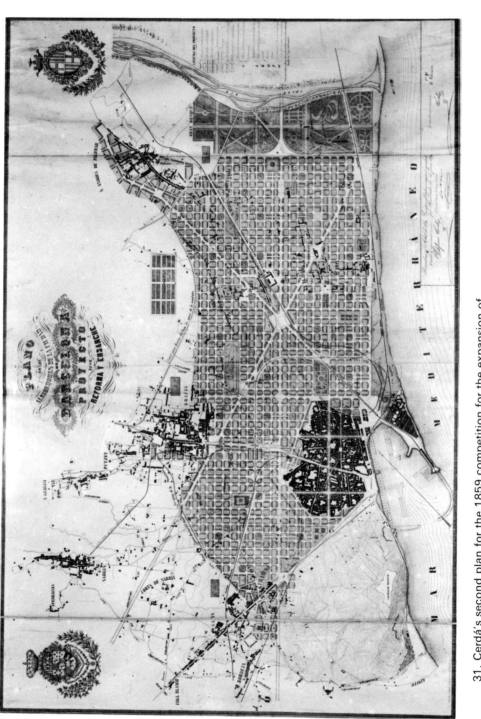

31. Cerdá's second plan for the 1859 competition for the expansion of Barcelona. There is considerably more variation in the directions of the two-sided blocks here than in his first design in which they were arranged more as corridors.

32. Plaza de Cataluña, Barcelona, at the beginning of the twentieth century.

34. Dresden-Neustadt, in 1879.

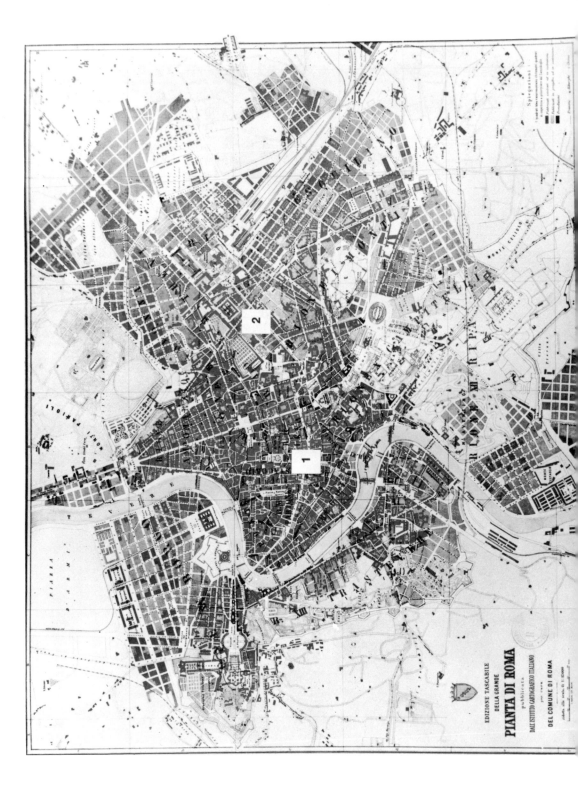

EDIZIONE TASCABILE
DELLA GRANDE

PIANTA DI ROMA

pubblicata

DALL'ISTITUTO CARTOGRAFICO ITALIANO

per cura

DEL COMUNE DI ROMA

ridotta alla scala di 1:12500

1- Corso Vittorio Emanuele; 2- Via Nazionale.

36. San Francisco in the 1850's, showing the juxtaposition of the grid plans.

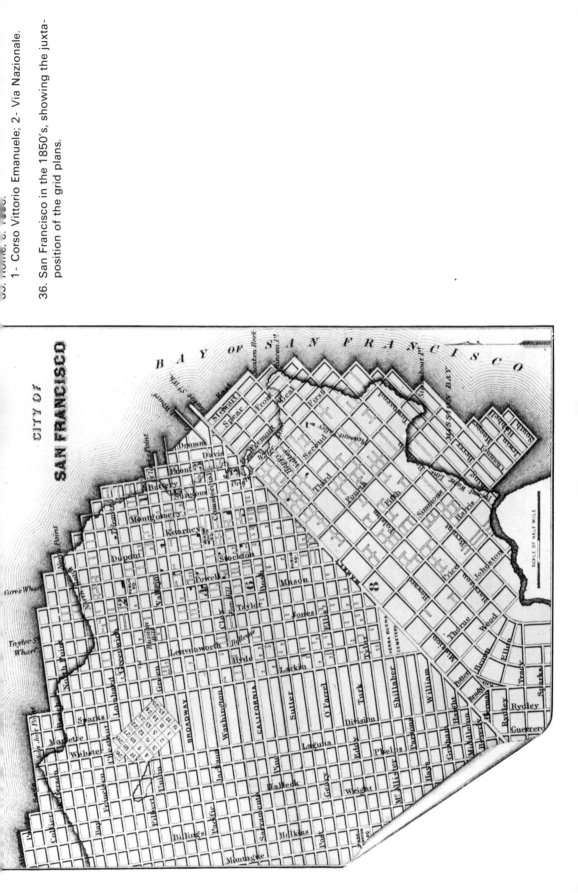

37. Chicago, in 1855.

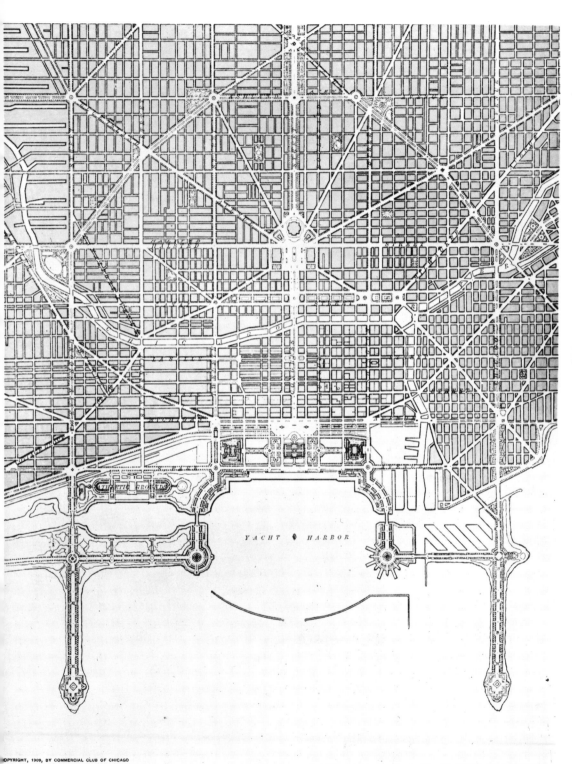

YACHT ⬥ HARBOR

CX. CHICAGO. PLAN OF THE COMPLETE SYSTEM OF STREET CIRCULATION; RAILWAY STATIONS; PARKS, BOULEVARD CIRCUITS AND RADIAL ARTERIES; PUBLIC RECREATION PIERS, YACHT HARBOR, AND PLEASURE–BOAT PIERS; TREATMENT OF GRANT PARK; THE MAIN AXIS AND THE CIVIC CENTER, PRESENTING THE CITY AS A COMPLETE ORGANISM IN WHICH ALL ITS FUNCTIONS ARE RELATED ONE TO ANOTHER IN SUCH A MANNER THAT IT WILL BECOME A UNIT.

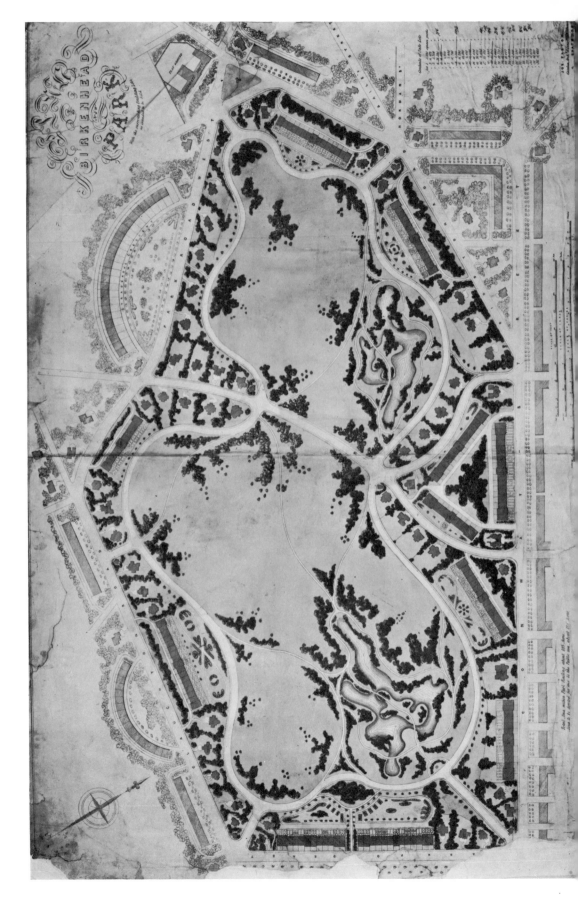

designed by Joseph Paxton in 1844.

40. Looking north over Central Park in New York City as seen in a lithograph of 1863 by John Bachmann.

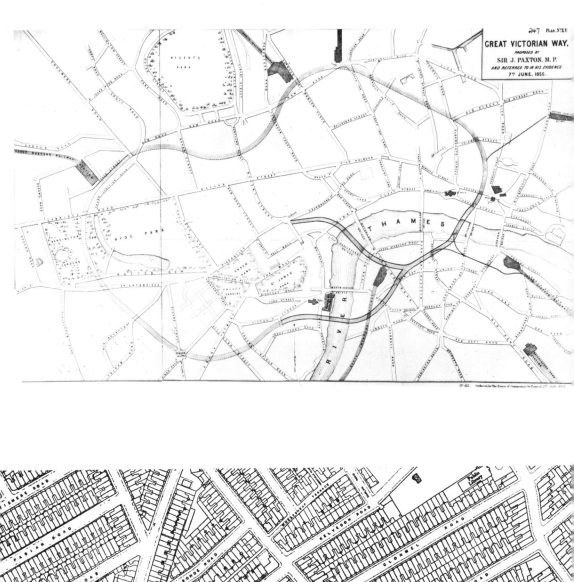

GREAT VICTORIAN WAY,

PROPOSED BY

SIR J. PAXTON. M.P.

AND REFERRED TO IN HIS EVIDENCE

7TH JUNE. 1855.

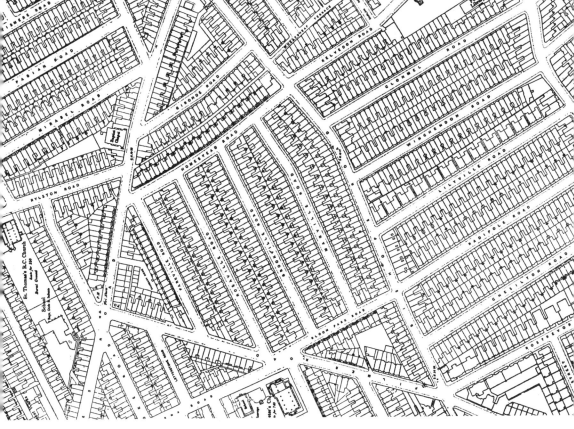

41. Paxton's project for the Great Victorian Way circling central London, 1855.

42. An example of metropolitan housing according to London's bylaws. Raymond Unwin, publishing this in 1909, remarked: "The truth is that in this work we have neglected the amenities of life. We have forgotten that endless rows of brick boxes, looking out on dreary streets and squalid backyards, are not really homes for people, and can never become such, however complete may be the drainage system, however pure the water supply, or however detailed the bye-laws under which they are built." (*Town Planning in Practice*, p. 4).

43. Perspective view of the park-settlement of Le Vésinet, 1858.

44. Plan of Bedford Park, Chiswick, drawn in 1896.

45. Hampstead Garden Suburb, designed by Barry Parker and Sir Raymond Unwin, 1907.

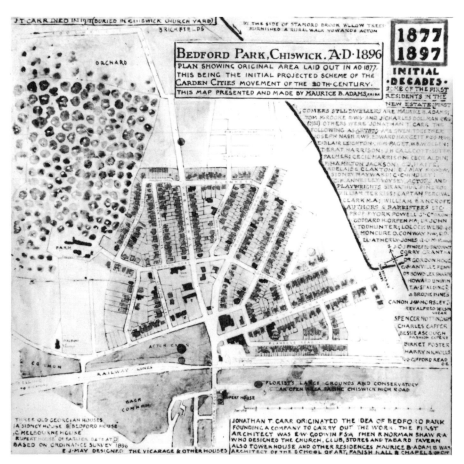

1- brook; 2- woods; 3- golf course; 4- Finchley Road; 5- Central Square; 6- shopping center; 7- Asmuns Place; 8- Hampstead Way.

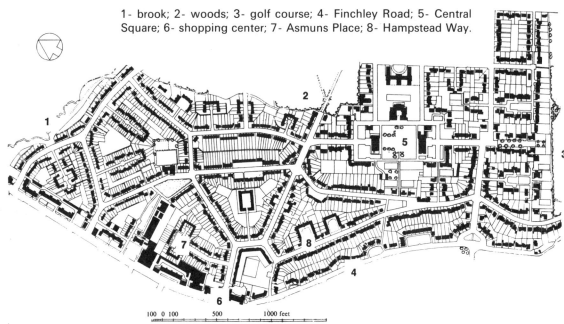

46. Bird's-eye view of the workers' colonies at Mulhouse, 1855.

47. Pullman, City, Illinois. Panorama in 1893.

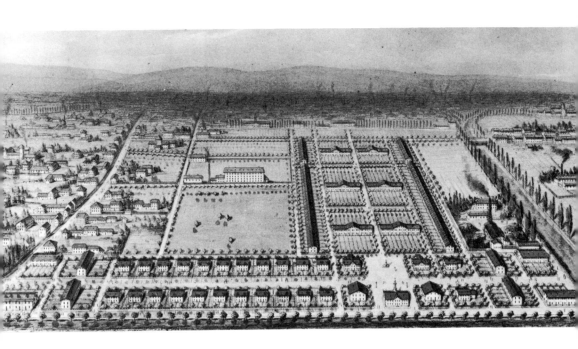

48. Bournville, 1879, for the Cadbury Chocolate Works (from a map of 1897 by A. P. Walker). The first houses are at the lower left, facing Linden Road.

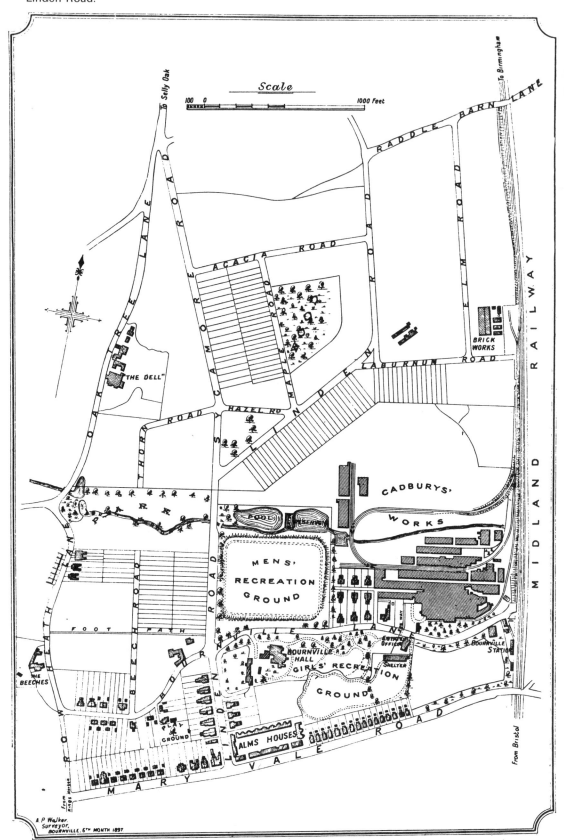

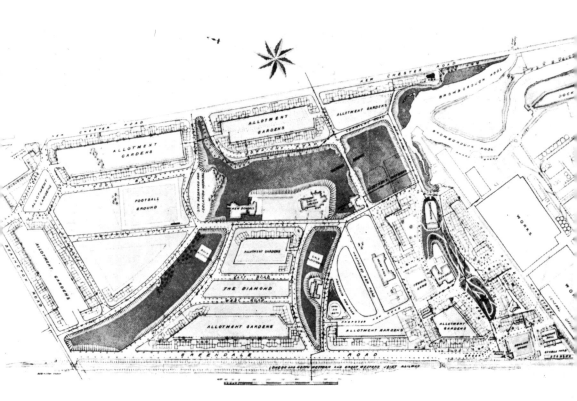

49. Port Sunlight, built for Lord Leverhulme, 1888. The earliest part is at lower right in this plan of the early 1900's.

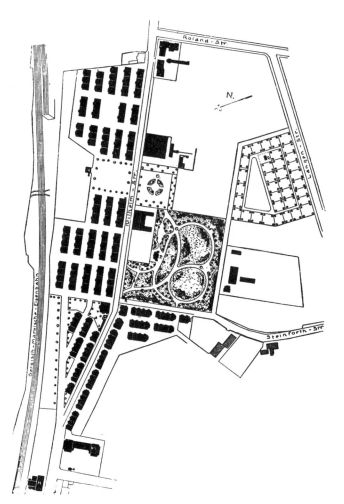

50. Krupp workers' colony of Schederhof, Essen, in 1872–1873.

51. Krupp colony of Alfredshof 1, Essen, as originally laid out in 1894.

52. Detail of the Krupp colony of Atenhof, Essen.

53. Krupp colony of Alfredshof 2, Essen,
   as extended.

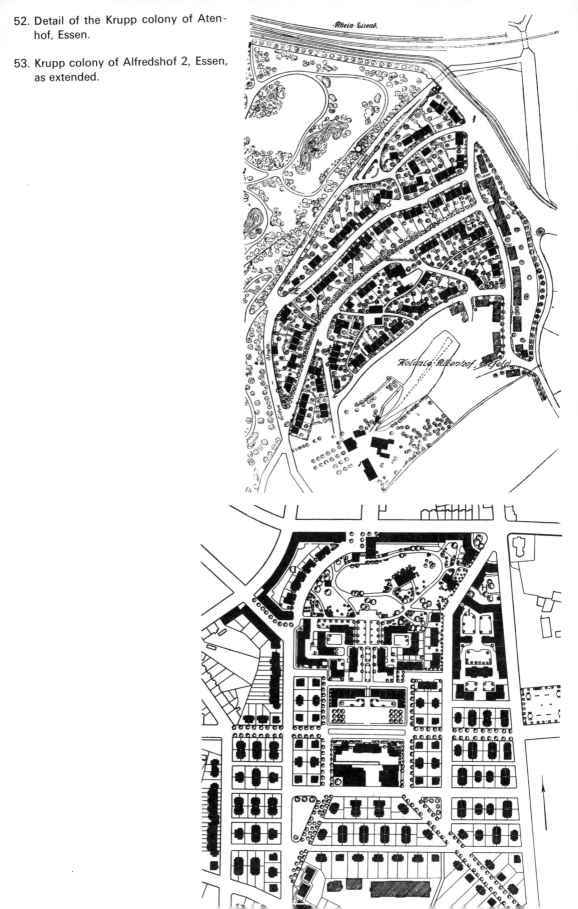

54. Agneta Park in Delft, 1880.
   A. Coffee house
   B. Supermarket and bakery
   C. Director's residence
   D. Community school
   E. Labor union
   F. Children's playground
   G. Music pavilion
   H. Boat shed

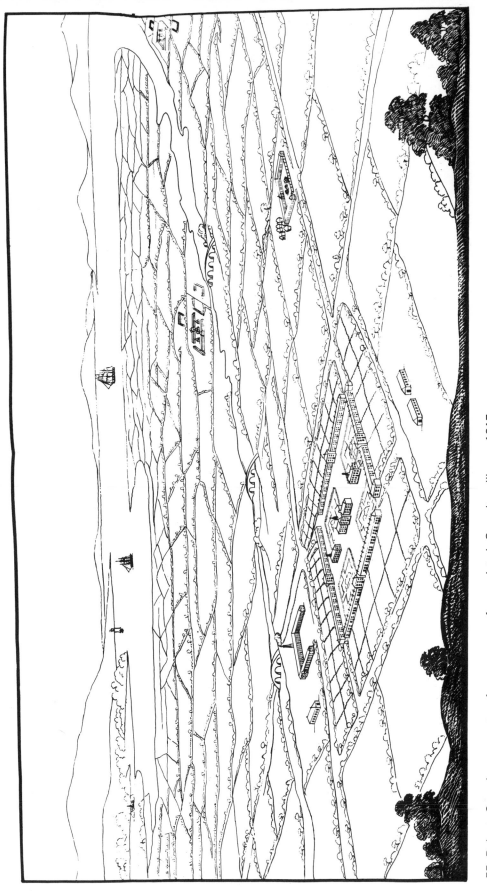

55. Robert Owen's prospectus for a group of associated Owenite villages, 1817.

56. Rendering by Stedman Whitwell, Owen's architect, of a single Owenite community, c. 1826.

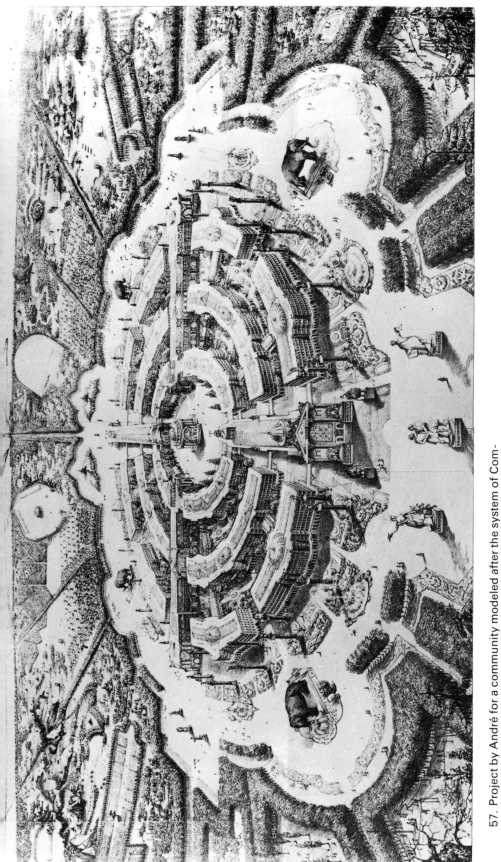

57. Project by André for a community modeled after the system of Communaute, based on equality, liberty, fraternity, unity—the eternal principles which may result in happiness. It was not uncommon for social utopias of the nineteenth century to take on forms reminiscent of geometric ideal cities of the Renaissance.

58. Panoramic view of a *phalanstère* organized according to Fourier's
    theory, 1847.

59. Main building of a projected Fourierist *phalanstère*.

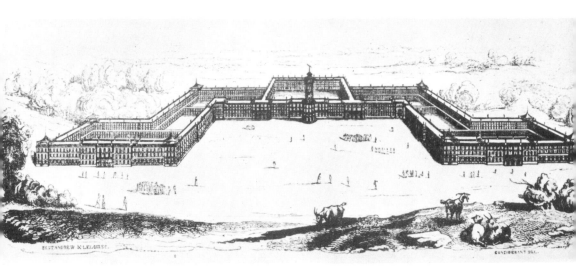

60. Guise. *Familistère* or Social Palace with the Godin plant, 1871.

61. Guise. Plan of the *familistère*.

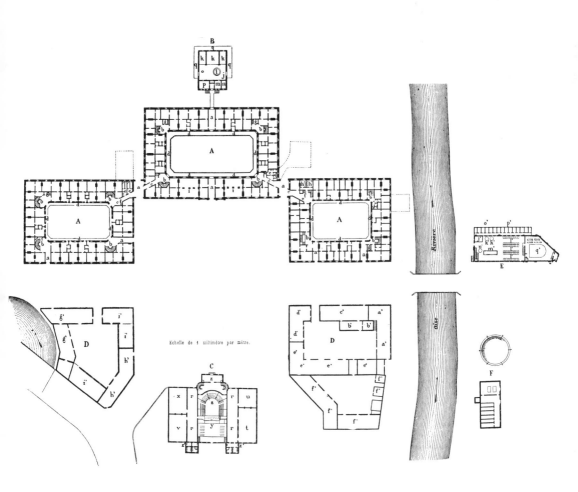

62. Theory of the linear city, uniting old *point cities*, Arturo Soria y Mata, 1880's.

63. Bird's-eye view of an ideal linear city of the Soria type.

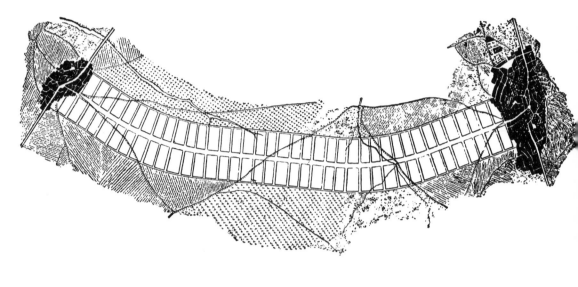

64. Cross-section of the main artery of the first portion of the Ciudad Lineal in Madrid.

65. Layout of actual Ciudad Lineal of Madrid in relation to the center of Madrid (at lower left), 1894.

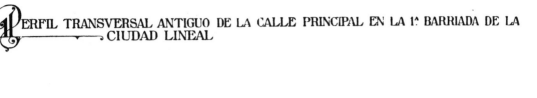

PERFIL TRANSVERSAL ANTIGUO DE LA CALLE PRINCIPAL EN LA 1ª BARRIADA DE LA CIUDAD LINEAL

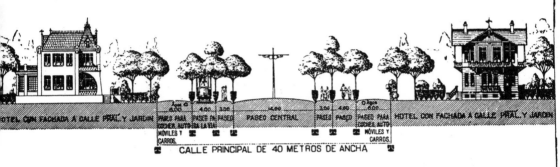

CALLE PRINCIPAL DE 40 METROS DE ANCHA

Viaje de Puerta del Sol á Ciudad Lineal.

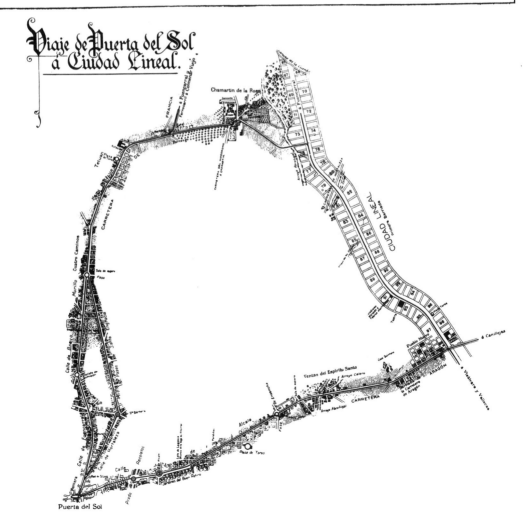

Puerta del Sol

66. Schematic layout of the cité industrielle by Tony Garnier.

67. Perspective view of the hospital area in Garnier's cité.

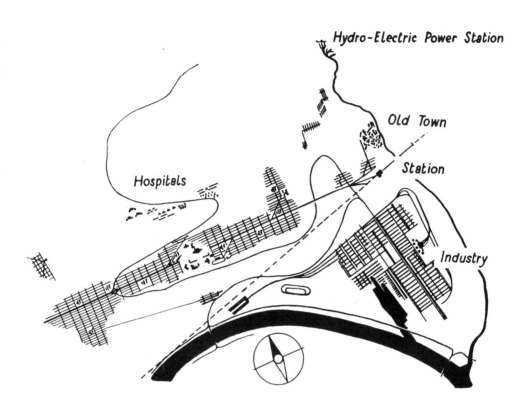

Hydro-Electric Power Station

Old Town

Station

Hospitals

Industry

70. John Ruskin finds the culturalist model of a city in the old towns of Europe (Zug, 1835), and anticipates the later theories of William Morris and, to a certain extent, Camillo Sitte.

71. Camillo Sitte: Padua, Piazza del Duomo (I).

72. Sitte: Parma.
   I- Piazza della Steccata; II- Piazza Grande (Garibaldi); a- Palazzo Comunale (de Governatore); b- Madonna della Steccata; c- Palazzo della Podestería (del Municipo).

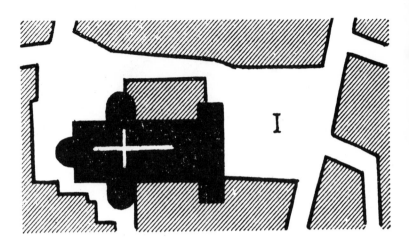

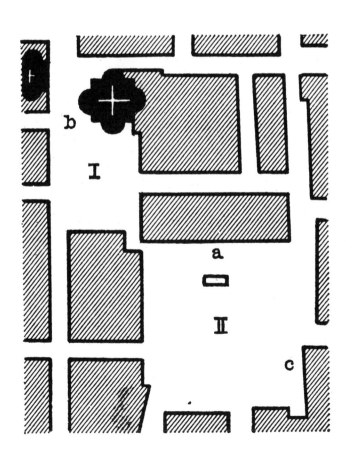

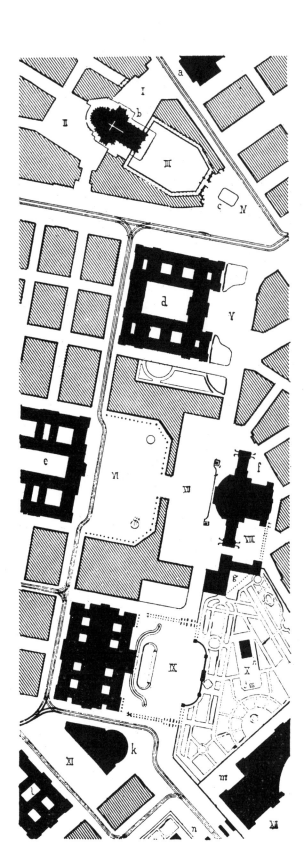

73. Sitte: Suggestion for western portion of th
Vienna Ring.

Public Squares: I, II, IV- new plazas aroun
the Votive Church; III- atrium of the Votiv
Church; V- university plaza; VI- Rathau
plaza; VII- larger theater plaza; VIII- smalle
theater plaza; IX- plaza in front of Parliamer
building; X- plaza in the ·Volksgarten; XI
plaza in front of the Palace of Justice; XII
new Hofburg plaza.

Buildings: a- chemical laboratory; b- Votiv
Church; c- site for a large monument; d- uni
versity; e- Rathaus; f- Burgtheater; g- pro
jected new building related to Burgtheate
h- Temple of Theseus; j- suggested site fc
the Goethe Monument; k- an as yet unas
signed new building; 1- Palace of Justic
m- new Hofburg construction; n- projecte
triumphal arch.

74. Sitte: Project for the transformation monument of the Votive Church plaza, adding buildings G, H, J, monument K, and plazas E and F.

75. Sitte: Project for rearrangement of the Rathaus area (VI and VII in Fig. 73) so as to articulate meaningless voids. A- Burgtheater; B- new structure suggested by Sitte; C- Volksgarten; D- Rathaus; E and F- new buildings planned by Sitte.

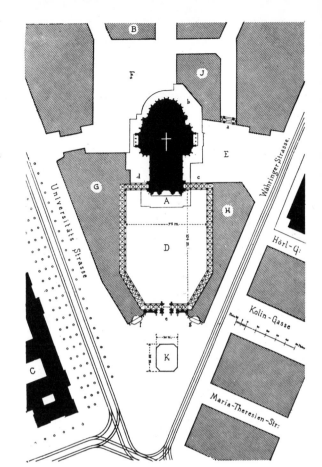

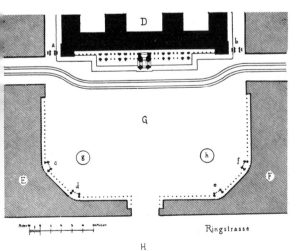

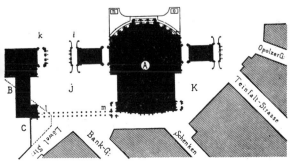

76. Plan for an extension of Flensburg, Germany, by Karl Henrici.

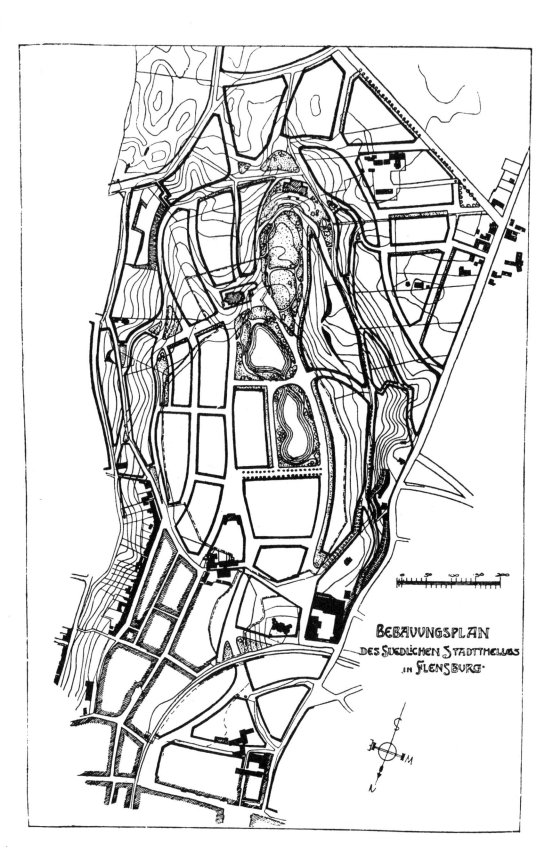

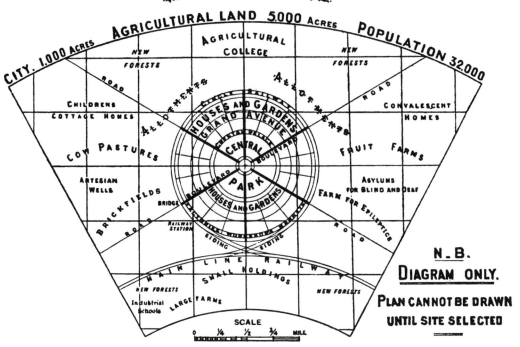

GARDEN CITY AND RURAL BELT

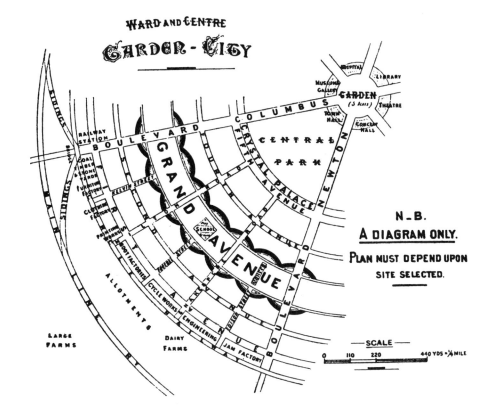

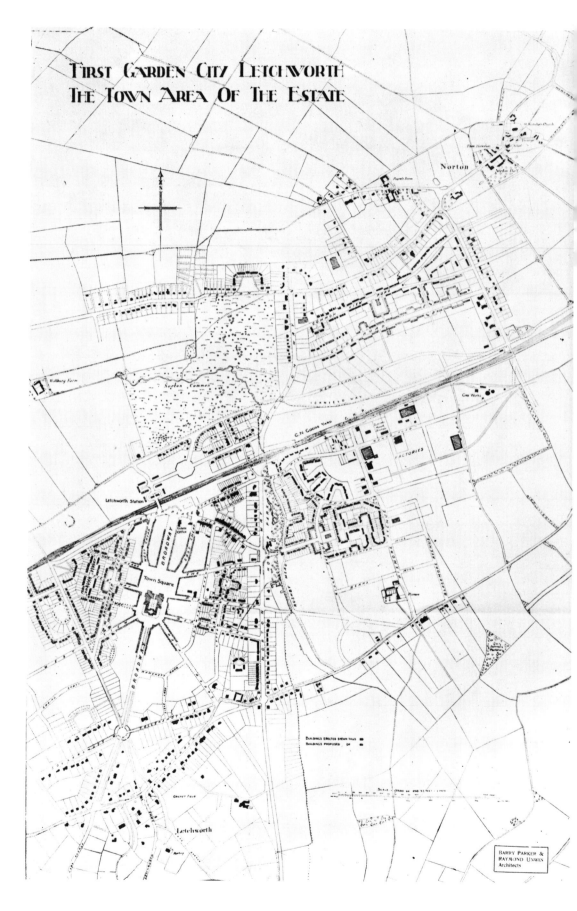

80. Letchworth. Bird's Hill area with its irregular layout of houses. The houses are arranged to afford the greatest number of countryside views.

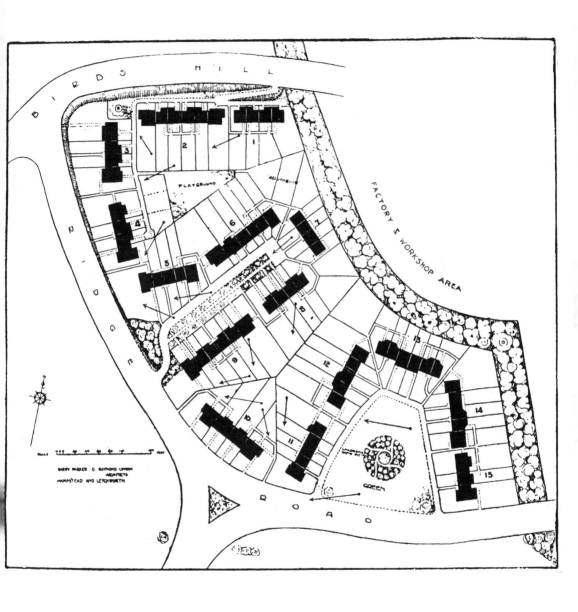

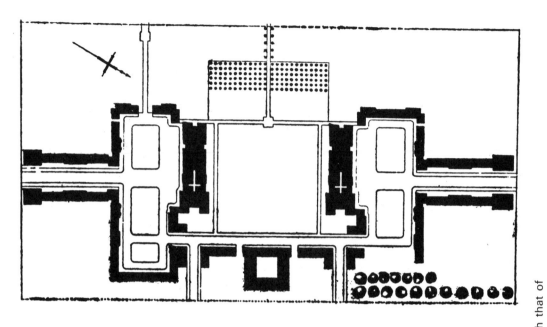

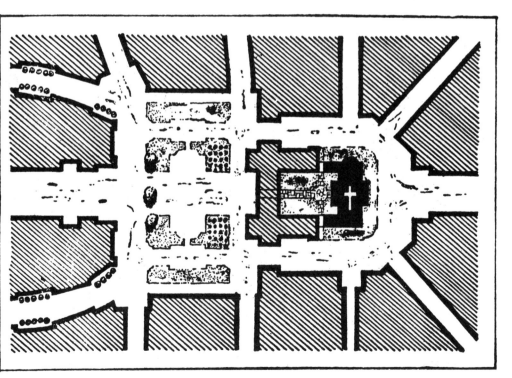

81. Comparison of the town square of Letchworth (left) with that of Hampstead Garden Suburb (right). Hampstead demonstrates the impact of the German Sittesque tradition of Unwin who was the

squares in quadrilateral formation (*Fig. 59*). Richardson, who reserved separate districts for public buildings, hospitals, hydrotherapeutic establishments, and laundries, also envisioned a building area where "each workman can have a work-room on payment of a moderate sum per week [and where] he may work as many hours as he pleases... the family is thus separated from the work."[43]

However, unlike the case of language or other semiotic systems, there remains only a slight diversity in the associated elements of these projects. Here identity[44] tends to become the prerequisite for association. The concept of *prototype* which seemed to satisfy their egalitarian and economic aspirations haunted the progressists under the name of *model*. Victor Considérant (1808–1893), following the example of Fourier, proposes that "a new type of housing" be worked out.[45] Cabet is convinced of the necessity for a standard model of housing as, "all citizens should be housed in the same way and as well as possible." And he carries the idea to an extreme; not content with establishing a definitive prototype at Icara for each building category (housing, school, store, city hall), he even standardized apartments and furniture.[46]

With all these theorists, the major study is devoted to standardized housing. The small individual house finds its perfected model in Richardson's *Hygeia* (not to be confused with *Fig. 1*): it has a roof terrace, laboratory-kitchen on the top floor, rooms for hydrotherapy and storage, and it totally rejects decoration, bringing to mind the experiments of the 1920's. The collective solution, on the other hand, inspired an entirely new prototype in which space was also analyzed and classified: Fourier's *phalanstère* or Social Palace (*Fig. 59*), a unit of housing for two thousand people. Formally it is patterned on the anachronistic archetype of the Château of Versailles (*Fig. 59*), but this should not make us forget the originality of its interior economy and program. Actually the palace incorporates at the same time apartments (in the center and especially in the wings) which vary according to the income of the inhabitants and the size of families and facilities and nurseries. Common facilities, placed at the center of the buildings, included. kitchens, dining halls, laundries, baths, assembly, reception and concert halls, and a ballroom, while in dependent wings were nurseries, schools, workshops and hotels. A glassed-in street gallery on three levels, "one of the most characteristic 'organs'... connects all the parts of the whole," both public and private, and serves as an ideal sheltered meeting place. In the 1920's, the same conception will be taken up by avant-garde Soviet architects, who will be able to integrate it, at this time, into a relevant architectural space.[47]

Interconnections between model elements and model quarters follow a simple geometric order which strictly precludes the picturesque. The right angle acquires an almost mystical value, and the straight line symbolizes the break with the past and the advent of reason. Much more than the regularizing planners, the pre-urbanists are prepared to make a clean sweep of the past. For them geometry means truth as well as beauty. The problem of circulation is simplified by general classification of other functions. Except in the case of Icara, where streets "with eight tracks" served to distribute the means of locomotion, the street and circulation problem is essentially centered on protection from the elements; the main concern is to enable pedestrians to move about under shelter from bad weather—in covered passages at Icara, or in Fourier's famous street-gallery.

The importance of empty spaces and greenery, together with the division into independent functional units of two thousand like Owen's *square* and the *phalanstère*, leads to a loss of urban character in the progressist agglomerations. The traditional *city* disintegrates. The new plan has no boundaries; it is made up of endlessly juxtaposable standard units and represents a first step in the gradual suppression of the difference between town and country.

What then is the significance of the progressist model? It is the same as that of regularization insofar as the latter is history-conscious and aims at economic efficiency. For the progressist, however, economic efficiency is no more an end in itself. Progressist ordering is no longer monosemantical; it attempts to recover semantical richness by referring explicitly and not merely implicitly to an ideology which may be defined in terms of two conceptions of men and reason.

This optimistic attitude, the heritage of the Age of Enlightenment, considers that reason is the supreme value, to be discovered in the world and developed in man. "A new era must commence; the human intellect, through the whole extent of the earth, hitherto enveloped by the grossest ignorance and superstition, must begin to be released from its state of darkness.... For the time is come when the means may be prepared to train all the nations of the world—men of every color and climate, of the most diversified habits—in that knowledge...," wrote Owen.[48]

Hence the importance of the idea of a model, which is linked with both the conception of a universal human archetype and with a faith in the power of reason to determine scientifically and a-priori a framework for human behavior. Considérent defined his task in almost the same terms as were used later by Le Corbusier: "Consider man, his needs, tastes, and active inclinations in order to determine the conditions for the system of construction best adapted to his nature."[49]

This faith in reason is at once the greatness and limitation of the progressist model. It is great insofar as it consciously assumed a formative role and reflected the will to eradicate social inequality. In this respect it is the birth certificate of functionalism. However, as a corollary of its aspirations toward the universal and its rejection of syntagm and difference, the progressist model condemned itself to remain a rudimentary and repetitious system. Owing, moreover, to its educational vocation and abstract character, it also exercised repression. From a psychoanalytic point of view, it can be associated with the threatening father image as embodied in both Owen and Icara.

Certain Socialists tried to realize their utopias. Owen founded New Harmony in Indiana in 1825,[50] and Cabet organized settlements, first in Texas, in 1848, and later in Iowa, in 1853. Cabet's purpose was "to make an experiment in the interest of humanity in order to determine the system of social and political organization... most conducive to progress" to "experience the system described in *The Voyage in Icaria.*" These experiments were all carried out on too restricted a scale[51] and in a politically and economically unfavorable context, and were consequently doomed to failure.

The only lasting achievement, inspired by Fourierism, was the *familistère*, designed by the industrialist Jean Baptiste Godin (1817–1888) for his workers in Guise; it is still operating today (*Figs. 60–61*). Godin drew up the plan himself, and by 1859 construction had begun. In 1865, the Social Palace was occupied and achieved immediate fame.[52]

PROGRESSIST URBANISM

Toward the end of the nineteenth century, the progressist model undergoes a new phase of theoretical elaboration. However, owing to an evolution in the power structure, this phase is followed by an extensive practical achievement. On its own the liberal bourgeoisie sponsors the model of the progressist city. Unlike the apolitical second generation of specialists (following World War I), the two outstanding figures of the first generation of urbanists (before 1914) remained involved, though to a lesser degree than the pre-urbanists, with progressist political ideology. Arturo Soria y Mata (1844–1920) was a Spanish Republican and Tony Garnier (1869–1948) was appointed as chief architect of the city of Lyon by its Radical Socialist mayor, E. Herriot.

Soria started out as a theoretician of communication,[53] a

politician, philosopher and journalist, but later turned his full attention to urban and suburban traffic problems, and in particular to streetcars, establishing one of the first trolley lines in Madrid. Rapid urban transit by rail was, in fact, the basis of his idea for the *linear city*, (*La ciudad lineal*), which he began to develop in 1882 in a series of articles for the newspaper *El Progreso*.[54] In terms that recall Cerdá's, he wrote, "The form of the city is, or must be, derived from the necessities of locomotion."[55] George Collins has pointed out that he was "the first person in modern times to evolve a planning method based primarily on the transportation of physical objects and the transmission of public utilities."[56]

From his first article it is evident that Soria has already formed a total vision: "A single street of 500 meters' width and of the *length that may be necessary*—such will be the city of the future, whose extremities could be Cadiz and St. Petersburg, or Peking and Brussels [*Figs. 62–63*].

"Put in the center of this immense belt trains and trams, conduits for water, gas and electricity, reservoirs, gardens and, at intervals, buildings for different municipal services—fire, sanitation, health, police, etc.—and there would be resolved at once almost all the complex problems that are produced by the massive populations of our urban life.

"Our projected city unites the hygienic conditions of country life to the great capital cities...."[57]

Details will come afterward: along two parallel strips on either side of the spinal column, units designed for housing, work, and recreation would spread out, intermingled and unclassified, but interconnected by secondary streets perpendicular to the main thoroughfare. Soria is a fanatic believer in the othogonal.[58] Housing takes the form of individual units, designed to occupy, independently, one fifth of each allotted portion of residential land.

Space in the *ciudad lineal* has the same characteristics as in the progressist model; it is conceived a-priori as standardized, open, and functional. If Soria recommends mixing functions, it is perhaps because of the limitation imposed by the narrowness of his layout, to which he had assigned an essentially longitudinal organization based on the importance of traffic flow. At any rate, he abolishes the usual continuity between constructed elements and he standardizes housing. And finally, his linear structure, which afforded to the cities unlimited possibility of extension as well as the proximity to the countryside, tends at the same time to deprive it of a truly urban atmosphere.

Soria confidently defended his plan in numerous lectures and in a periodical entitled *La Ciudad Lineal*, which ran for nearly thirty-five years. He considered it to be universally applicable in any one of three forms: a ring around an already existing city, a ribbon running through an unpopulated area and connecting two cities (from Algeciras to Gibraltar, for example), or an entirely new town in an unurbanized region like the Andalusian or the Catalan coast. He was to apply his theory in the environs of Madrid, where the foundation of his Compañiá Madrileña de Urbanización, in 1894 allowed him the opportunity to build a linear town composed of superblocks of individual houses with their gardens along a central trolley line and roadway (*Figs. 64–65*).

The *ciudad lineal* has been more easily ignored by the second generation of progressist urbanists, since it came from an industrially backward country afflicted with social problems. It has also been more consciously ignored since Soria's idea was to be completely misappropriated. In his proposal for an industrial linear town, Le Corbusier simply *lifted* Soria's solution.

The *cité industrielle*, designed by Tony Garnier, a young winner of the *Prix de Rome*, during his stay at the Villa Medici between 1899 and 1901, had an altogether different organization, with stricter zoning and a less abstract structure. From the outset, Garnier limited his population to 35,000 inhabitants and picked out a specific geographic region, namely southeastern France, in the vicinity of Rive de Gier, St.-Etienne, St.-Chamond: because of these specifications, elementary as they may seem, the *cité industrielle* must be considered as an illustration of progressist spatial distribution rather than a universal model.

In accordance with Garnier's classification of space, industrial establishments are spread out along the river, near a hydroelectric plant fed by a waterfall, whereas the city proper is located on a plateau and the sanitary installations on a still higher level (*Figs. 66–67*). These zones were to be discontinuous, expandable, and separated by areas of greenery. Public buildings, generally classified as administrative services, assembly halls, sports and entertainment centers, were broken down into still finer categories and placed in the central area of the *city*. Houses and schools, on the other hand, were located along the periphery. These constructed elements were implanted along continuous stretches of greenery intersected by an orthogonal street network (*Figs. 68–69*).

Tony Garnier's city was the first major urbanist project to propose prototypal forms corresponding to the new conception of space. Soria was not concerned with architectural and esthetic considerations; Garnier, on the other hand, designed houses with terraces and atriums, apartment buildings mounted on pilotis, and public halls with reinforced-concrete mushroom

columns. All this was to stir the imagination of a whole generation of architects and introduce them to a new esthetic in city
planning. Le Corbusier, who admittedly learned a great deal
from the example of Garnier's project, saw in it "an attempt to
establish order and combine utilitarian and plastic solutions...
the selection of essential volumes and spaces [designed] in
accordance with practical necessity and the demands of that
poetic sense which is peculiar to the architect."[59]

PRE-URBANISM AND URBANISM:
THE CULTURALIST MODEL

PRE-URBANISM

The culturalist model took shape after the progressist one and
unlike the latter emerged not from a revolutionary vision but
from criticism of an existing urban situation which was now
more thoroughly entrenched.

The new model was retrospective in that it clung to the coher-
ent and exemplary image of the preindustrial city in opposition
to the contemporary image of urban incoherence. Underlying it
was a new form of nostalgia which had awakened gradually
with the development of historical studies at the end of the
eighteenth century and with the application of historical
perspective to the study of art and culture. Hegel made a first
description of the perfect cultural whole embodied by the ancient
Greek city, stressing its formative role. During the remainder of
the century, historians such as Michelet, Burckhardt, and Fustel
de Coulanges compared the disunity of the preindustrial city
with the tightly knit cultural communities of the Middle Ages,
the Italian Renaissance and ancient Rome. From this period date
the concepts of the organic and the mechanical, [60] which were
evolved to contrast the functioning of the past with that of the
present. Romantic esthetics linked them with beauty and
ugliness, respectively. Later they were given more precision by
Max Weber in terms of the dichotomy *Gemeinschaft-Gesell-
schaft*.

Though a whole segment of nineteenth-century European
thought nostalgically analyzed the beautiful organic wholes of
the past, only Great Britain was to set them up as models, notably
in the writings of John Ruskin (1818–1900) and William
Morris (1834–1896). This circumstance may be attributed to
the force of tradition in Great Britain, and to the fact that as the
pioneer in industrialism, she was also one of its most mutilated

102

victims. In France, Victor Hugo weeps over the same image of the past as do Ruskin and Morris, but he does not project it into the future. "Let there be no mistake," he wrote, "architecture is dead, hopelessly dead, killed by the printed word. Imagine what an investment would be required to rewrite the architectural book. Humanity's great poem, her great edifice, will not be rebuilt, it will be printed."[61] As for Viollet le Duc (1814–1879), he analyzes the system of Gothic architecture, but only to hold it up to modern technicians as an example of rational structure. Neither outlook was in any way comparable to that of A. W. N. Pugin (1812–1852), who, as the instigator of the Gothic Revival, was to inspire Ruskin. Pugin's purpose was to recapture, through architectural activity, the overall process of an organic society.

For Ruskin and Morris alike, recovery of the urban order of the past represented a way of recovering, through a kind of catharsis, the spiritual values on which rested the past communities. Their model, implicit in Ruskin's work and explicit in Morris' description of the twenty-first-century Europe is patterned, by means of critical analysis, on the features of old towns like Rouen, Oxford, or Venice (*Fig. 70*). It can be contrasted point by point with the progressist model.

The culturalist city has well-defined limits. There are no more tentacular suburbs. When the hero of Morris' *News from Nowhere* returns to the site of old London, he no longer recognizes the city, which has grown smaller; peripheral slum and industrial areas as well as residential sprawl have been suppressed; London is once again surrounded by beautiful countryside. Culturalist cities are small and concentrated: consequently, their urban fabric is continuous. Yet within the close-woven fabric, variety, irregularity, and asymmetry prevail: standardization is condemned. After counting 678 identical windows on the same side of Queen Street, Ruskin asked the inhabitants of Edinburgh: "You do not feel interested in *hearing* the same thing over and over again;—why do you suppose you can feel interested in seeing the same thing over and over again?"[62] His demand for diversity is justified by the variety found in nature; each individual should be free to express his own vital reality by growing, as it were his individual shell. The culturalist city derived its significance from the variety of facades whose gables and openings are never identically designed and form the contrast between private buildings and the grander, more sumptuous civic buildings. In this model, organic beauty, the fruit of man's patient handiwork, assumes the importance attributed to hygiene in the progressist model.

The culturalist model cannot be considered as reactionary,

nor even as a conservative utopia in Karl Mannheim's sense. For behind it lay the hope of developing an unalienated man who would no more be the simple rational being of the progressists but a complete person. Morris clearly stated: "the Fourierist phalansteries and all their kind, as was but natural at the time, implied nothing but a refuge from mere destitution."[63] Satisfaction of material needs is not enough. The goal of the socialist Morris is the development of a popular culture. "The cause of art is the cause of the people."[64]

Nonetheless, the culturalist vision has a negative side: whatever the denials of Morris, who did not wish to be a "mere railer against progress" and perceived "amidst all this filth of civilization the seeds of a great change," it fails to acknowledge the irreversible nature of the mutation which the Industrial Revolution had engendered.[65] In psychoanalytical terms, the culturalist model is associated with the comforting image of the maternal breast; it is regressive.

URBANISM—CAMILLO SITTE

It is Camillo Sitte (1843–1903) who makes the transition from pre-urbanism to urbanism in the culturalist model. In his book, *Der Städte-Bau nach seinen künstlerischen Grundsätzen*, he gives the culturalist model a more complex and precise structure which will eventually lead to its practical application.

Sitte, director of the State School of Industrial Arts in Vienna since 1883 and also an erudite professor of art history, remains primarily an architect. He posesses the technical skill that both Ruskin and Morris lacked, but is devoid of the political social involvement that motivated their work. Esthetics are his guiding principle.

Sitte's book has its origin in the contemporary attempts at modernizing Vienna, and in particular, construction of the Ring, which was taking place practically before his eyes and offered an example of what not to do. In order to indicate the right directions, he elaborated a model of spatial organization based on systematic analysis—"in a purely artistic and technical manner," of the "compositional elements" which came into play in the preindustrial city and evolved from an innate, instinctive aesthetic sense."[66] Pencil in hand and working from books, but more often *in situ* during the course of frequent travels, Sitte dissected classical, medieval, and baroque spatial organization.

In all three types, one can find the same fundamentals which are inherent in the connection of their elements. Space is continuous, and buildings have meaning only insofar as they are related to each other; for Sitte "the modern disease of isolated construction" is to be condemned and monuments are actually to be built into the urban fabric: on ancient European plazas, for example, churches were seldom entirely disengaged from adjacent buildings on more than one side (*Figs. 71–72*). Hence, also, the importance and value given to connecting elements such as plazas and streets which modern planning can conceive of only in terms of voids: "Plazas used to form a whole with their surrounding buildings," wrote Sitte. "...in the Middle Ages and the Renaissance there still existed a vital and functional use of the town square for community life and also, in connection with this, a rapport between square and surrounding public buildings. Meanwhile in our day plazas are, at most, used as parking lots."[67]

What is more, to function effectively, urban space should be enclosed. "...The main requirement for a plaza, as for a room, is the enclosed character of its space."[68] Enclosure is also considered by Sitte as essential to a feeling of well-being. Analysis shows that access streets leading off like turbine blades contribute to the closed-in feeling that is characteristic of ancient plazas. In this spirit, the Viennese planner considers areas of greenery to be like plazas, carefully circumscribing them with buildings in order to keep them from losing their urban character.

In the distribution of solids and voids, the only criteria should be irregularity, imagination, and asymmetry. This is to condemn the straight line, regularity, and symmetry which have led modern planners to place statues and fountains at the center of a plaza and not, as in the past, along its edge.

The first practical instance to which Sitte applies his analysis is in connection with a project for the Ring[69] (*Fig. 73*). In the area of the Votive Church, for example, Sitte confronts the problem of an inert, unified space in which disparate edifices (church, university and a chemical laboratory) stand out as isolated units (*Fig. 74*). He chooses to interconnect them by means of a series of arcades and new construction adjoining the church which will partition the area. Thus he obtains two new plazas and achieves limited vistas to avoid the former feeling of vacuousness; he attains intimate enclosures, human scale and a surprisingly rich network of walkways.

Hence the main features of the Sittesque spatial model are continuity in constructed elements, enclosure, diversity, asymmetry, irregularity, and connecting elements which are significant in themselves. Sitte for the first time radically challenges a-priori abstract city planning which comes off the drafting board, and points out its failure to take concrete experience into account. Thus he stresses the existential value of space and defines what might be called a behavioral space (*Fig. 75*). No wonder that Aristotle's word *security* appears on the first page of his book; his investigation into esthetic value in city planning should not be confused with the numerous contemporary tendencies toward two-dimensional pictorial effects.

The limitations of Sittesque planning arise, nonetheless, from the exclusive importance accorded the esthetic dimension, even when it is extended to include physical and psychological well-being. In his project for the Ring, for example, Sitte designs buildings and elaborates forms primarily for the purpose of arranging space and scarcely considers their meaning or their intended use. This purely esthetic approach became as mono-semantical as the economically determined planning of Hauss-mann. Sitte's model misses the fundamental destination of the modern city and ignores its complexity; it applies only to neighborhoods, on the level of the everyday activity of the pedestrian.

This explains, in fact, why it was used mainly in plans for suburban areas and for city extension. In this connection, as soon as his book was published Sitte's ideas were immediately and enthusiastically adopted in Germanic countries, where, as the Collinses have pointed out, they appealed to a latent nationalism and began to undermine the prevalent Haussmann-type planning. Following the publication of his book, several municipalities (Altona, Brünn, Linz, Olmütz) were to request Sitte or his collaborators as urbanist. The most important achievements based on Sittesque planning are by Karl Henrici (1842–1922) (*Fig. 76*), who planned the extension of Dessau (1890) and of Munich (1893); Theodor Fischer (1862–1938), the Chief Town Planner in Munich from 1893 on; Theodor Goecke (1850–1919), Otto Lasne (1854–1935), and Friedrich Puetzer (1871–1922) who worked in Darmstadt,[70] Wiesbaden, Mainz.

In Great Britain, Sitte exerted a strong influence, though not until the beginning of the twentieth century, when his cause was taken up by Patrick Geddes and Sir Raymond Unwin. On the other hand, in French-speaking countries where his book was translated in 1902, Sitte was almost completely ignored.[71] After World War I, the situation was aggravated by Le Corbusier when he stigmatized the Austrian planner as an apologist "for the donkey's way" and a "passé au petit pied."

Outside the specific realm of urban planning, Sitte's theories also apply to the conservation of old cities. Thanks to Sitte and his contemporary, Burgomaster Charles Buls (1837–1914), who was responsible for the restoration of the Grande Place in Brussels, a new objective was formulated: the preservation of an *urban ensemble* and its *fabric*.[72]

THE AMBIGUITIES OF THE GARDEN CITY

In 1898 the Socialist Ebenezer Howard (1850–1928) designed the Garden City, one of the last and most influential utopian models to come out of the nineteenth century. This model does not rely upon imagination nor does it provide a three-dimensional image; it consists of diagrams and their explanation.

Howard intends the Garden City as a refuge from the alienating character of the big city and a compensation for the deficiencies of country life. A new type of entity, it was to combine the social advantages of the city and the healthy conditions of rural areas.

The Garden City is limited in size and population. But it is autonomous and designed to incorporate all types of labor. It is encircled by an inalienable rural greenbelt. It encompasses an area of 6,000 acres, though only 1,000 acres (one sixth) were reserved for the city proper, which is conceived on a circular plan (*Fig. 77*). The radius of the city scarcely exceeds one-half mile, and its population must not exceed 32,000 inhabitants. In his diagram, Howard indicated that secondary and primary sectors (factories and agricultural activities) should be localized on the periphery, while the tertiary sector would be established in the center—with the main public buildings—around a navel-like park (*Fig. 78*). As soon as the population tends to exceed the specified maximum, a part forms a new nucleus, which will give birth to a new city. According to this process, Howard envisioned whole systems of Garden Cities, situated on the perimeters of large circles of ten-mile radius whose centers would be occupied by a mother city which might, on occasion, attain a population of 65,000 inhabitants. All these units are interconnected, and also connected to the mother city, through a system of rapid transit by electric rail.

The term *garden* has led to misinterpretation, and Howard's Garden Cities have often been confused with pseudurbias, as is the case with Georges Benoit-Lévy, whose plan for a garden city is actually a garden dormitory. Howard revealed his originality, in comparison with the paternalistic pseudurbia, in the creation of true, complete urban units in which all forms of human activity should be represented.

It is obvious that the Garden City has many features in common with the progressist model. Soria was not mistaken when he repeatedly compared it with his *ciudad lineal*, stressing in particular the objective common to both conceptions: *rus in urbe* (country in the city). It cannot be denied that physical hygiene was one of Howard's main preoccupations. Furthermore, he also recommends a kind of zoning, and he relates his satellite city to a transportation system.

The differences, however, are greater than the similarities. The Garden City is, in fact, a *particular version of the culturalist model*, primarily because of its precise limitation in space. Such Malthusian restraint is a prerequisite for the type of social life envisioned by Howard and for the development of individuals within a differentiated community. Moreover, as Soria well understood, Howard condemns standardization and encourages variety in the handling of space and building. The independent, individual house is permitted only on condition that it coexists with related constructions. Finally, the town-center has an urban atmosphere, and it may be said that the Garden City's productive relationship with the surrounding countryside recalls somewhat the role of countryside with respect to the medieval town, which Lewis Mumford described as "being of the country."[73]

The first Garden Cities actually created were evidence of this profound adherence to culturalism. Howard was a realist as well as a utopian. As early as 1899, he founded the Garden City Association, which enabled him to purchase the necessary land for Letchworth in 1903, where he undertook his first experiment, with Richard Barry Parker and Sir Raymond Unwin as architects (*Fig. 79*). Unwin, who was assigned the task of drafting the plan, used Howard's diagram but also borrowed heavily from Sitte: layouts for paths, intimacy in space, diversified buildings made to interrelate three-dimensionally (*Figs 80–81*). Unwin himself acknowledged how much he owed to preindustrial urban patterns in his esthetic treatment of space.

CONCLUSION

Along with the emergence of critical planning, the nineteenth century experienced a parallel development of urban studies that branched out into corrective sociology. In his studies of the European working class, Frédéric Le Play (1806–1882) demonstrated the relationship between the structural pattern of labor, family, and social groupings. Later, geographers brought to light the role that geohistorical factors play in the formation of cities, while the German school, with Friedrich Ratzel as its exponent, developed the science of urban ecology. In France, Elisée Reclus (1830–1905) stressed the unique personality of each city, taking up again and further elaborating the metaphor of the urban unit as a living organism; the dynamism of a city, he maintained, can be grasped and interpreted only through the annals of its history. Time plays a creative role, in accordance with Darwinian theory, and what was soon to be Bergsonism.

Out of an assimilation of these works, Patrick Geddes (1854–1932) evolved the *survey* method at the beginning of the twentieth century. But while this method acted as a corrective for urbanism by respecting the complexity of reality[74] and rejecting the a-priori, it was nevertheless used by Geddes within the context of a culturalist system of values and it remained dependent on the creative intervention of a planner. Consequently it did not fundamentally alter the course of critical planning.

Ultimately, regularization, pre-urbanism, and urbanism are the specific modes observable in urban planning for nineteenth-century industrial society. In their common departure from earlier procedures they share certain mutual traits.

First there is the agent of the break, namely self-conscious reflective process out of which came, through a series of problematic propositions, the actual concept of the city (and especially in the case of pre-urbanism and urbanism, the associated concept of countryside).

Secondly, there is the objectivising of urban space, for the first time conceived as a value in itself; a status made possible only by the semantic reduction to which the urban agglomeration was subjected as a consequence of the Industrial Revolution. Urban space ceases, in fact, to be implicitly related to significant social systems. This explains why city planning was preceded and accompanied by the development of metalanguages that justify, interpret, and in the last analysis, substantiate it. In all three phases, moreover, the urban project is thought out with reference to a systematic taxinomy more or less based on the idea of the city as an organism. The epistemological model, however, borrowed from the natural sciences, becomes increasingly involved with the matter of function.

The difference between the three approaches is essentially one of ideology or lack of ideology. *Regularization*, an analytical process, furthers the ends of the monosemantical industrial order, which neither Haussmann nor Olmsted question; they merely seek to give it a *good form*.

Pre-urbanism, on the contrary, is synthetic and based on a-priori reasoning; it relates its proposals to ideologies. Whether it opts for or opposes the values of industrial society, its models are fraught with justifications which provide compensation—an (unconscious) analogue of the lost polysemy. Ideology in the guise of a science, actually takes the place of former institutional systems.

Urbanism, a latecomer, since its first practical achievements date only from the 1890's, follows the two main courses charted by pre-urbanism. By this time, however, the urbanist-architect (Sitte, Unwin, Garnier) has arrived on the scene, and city planning has laid claim to being a science; as a result, the options underlying each of the orientations tend to become obscured. These developments make the reification of space complete.

Though cut off from their ideological roots, the two models born of pre-urbanism continued to survive well into the first half of the twentieth century. The progressist model been propagated, particularly by the Bauhaus, Le Corbusier and the rationalist architects of C.I.A.M. It was also developed during the 1920's in the Soviet Union, where, contrary to what occurred in other European countries, it was linked with revolutionary ideology; Fourier's housing unit as interpreted there by Moisei I. Ginzburg, acquired a meaning totally lacking in Le Corbusier's *Unitiés*. Also envisaged in Soviet Russia is Soria's linear city, which is looked upon as an ideal instrument for production.[75] As for the culturalist model, it has mainly been applied in the Anglo-Saxon world, viz. in England after World War II when it inspired the building of the New Towns.

With these models has persisted an anachronistic nineteenth-century outlook. No attempt has yet been made to psychoanalyze the choice of directions in urban planning, and even more seriously lacking is an epistemology of methods: metalanguages cannot be helped but they ought to be synchronized with the epistemology, the conceptual tools and processes of today. Modern planners still think in terms of classification and biological metaphors borrowed from the Lamarck-Darwinian thought approach. Up until World War II the idea of *system*, which is related to positivism, did not give way to that idea of *structure* which is necessary to keep pace with the other branches of science. In our day it would seem that this structural approach must be looked for in some form of regularizing urbanism that will remain abreast of the movement of history, and at the same time be open to creative innovation.

NOTES

THE CRITICAL ORDER

1. In his preface to *Les Bourgeois conquérants*, p. v.
2. In *Teoría general de Urbanización* (Madrid, 1867), Vol. 1, Part I, Introduction, p. 1.
3. F. de Saussure, one of the founders of structural linguistics, coined the word *semiology* (from the Greek *semeion*, "sign") to mean "a science which studies the life of signs in the midst of social life." For him, language (*la Langue*) as "a system of signs expressing ideas and thus comparable to writing, to the deaf and dumb's alphabet, to symbolical rites, to forms of politeness... is nothing but the most important among these various systems." But this *particular system* represents a kind of ideal type, from the study of which research in other fields of symbolical activity may be stimulated and developed. Saussure foresaw that "linguistics might become the general model of any semiology." Such was after him the point of linguists like E. Benvéniste or R. Jakobson. Some nonverbal semiological systems have actually been studied in this light by Claude Lévi-Strauss and R. Barthes. In his *Eléments de sémiologie* (see English translation as *Elements of Semiology*, published with *Writing Degree Zero*, London: Jonathan Cape, 1967), the latter indicates that "the aim of semiological research is to restore the functioning of systems of meaning other than language."
4. This word has been borrowed from the linguists who, following de Saussure, have differentiated two fundamental types of relationships between linguistic elements: to wit, spatial contiguity and similarity (which schematically correspond to two forms of mental activity: conjunction and association). Syntagm corresponds to the relationship of contiguity, paradigm to the relationship of similarity. From this double process, which one finds in all semiological systems, R. Jakobson has taken (borrowing from the field of rhetoric) the concepts of metaphor and metonymy which he uses to characterize the styles in the esthetic systems (literature, music and painting). Regarding our own use of the word *syntagmatic* (I could have used *metonymic*), it is considering that "placed in a syntagm, a term acquires its value only in opposition to preceding or following terms, or both." Barthes, *op. cit.*, p. 131.
5. With regard to crowding in the old city, Engels had this to say in *Die Lage der arbeitenden Klasse in England* "...the confusion has only recently reached its height when every scrap of space left by the old way of building has been filled up and patched over until not a foot of land is left to be further occupied." (English translation, p. 48.)
6. Concerning the absence of segregation of social classes in big French cities prior to the industrial era, see G. Duveau, *La vie ouvrière en France sous le Second Empire* (Paris: Gallimard, 1956). But then Engels in *Die Lage* remarks, "Every great city has one or more slums, where the working class is crowded together. True, poverty often dwells in hidden alleys close to the palaces of the rich; but in general, a separate territory has been assigned to it, where, removed from the sight of the happier class, it may struggle along as it can." (p. 26.) And, in Manchester, "by unconscious tacit agreement, as well as with outspoken conscious determination, the working people's quarters are sharply separated from the sections of the city reserved for the middle class." (p. 45.) Finally: "I have never seen so systematic a shutting out of the working class from the thoroughfares, so tender a concealment of everything which might affront the eye and the nerves of the bourgeoisie, as in Manchester." (p. 47.)
7. Edwin Chadwick speaking of Liverpool, Manchester, and Leeds; he echoes Victor Hugo, "I have descended into the cellars of Lille, I have seen these dark tombs."
8. Chapter 5 of Raymond Williams, *Culture and Society, 1780–1950* (New York: Doubleday and Company, 1958) contains an enlightening analysis of the Victorian industrial novels.
9. In connection with these pathological metaphors of the city one might mention the poetry of the Belgian Emile Verhaeren: *Les Campagnes Halluci-nées* of 1893 and *Les Villes tentaculaires* of 1895. These comparisons will outlive the nineteenth century and persist to our own day. To Le Corbusier,

Paris appears as a "cancer [which] is in good health," and he makes frequent use of Verhaeren's phrase, *tentacular cities*. Pierre Lavedan, in *Histoire de l'urbanisme* (Paris: Laurens, 1952), entitles the second chapter *The Sick City* and complains about the fact that "The history of the great cities of the nineteenth century is that of a disease." (p. 53.)

10. Engels, *Die Lage*, p. 48; *Saturday Review*, I, 1856.

11. *Description du Phalanstère et considérations sociales sur l'architectonique* (Paris: Libraire sociétaire), p. 40.

12. C. Morazé, *Les Bourgeois conquérants* (Paris: A. Colin, 1957), p. 204.

13. Lavedan, *op. cit.*, p. 13.

14. Olsen remarks incisively that "where the English have sought luxury and display, they have done so not in town, but in the country. The country house is the great architectural symbol of Post-Reformation English culture. The town was by comparison a machine for living which people used when they had to be in London." (*Town-Planning in London, the Eighteenth and Nineteenth Centuries*, New Haven: Yale University Press, 1964, p. 4.)

15. Lease lengths: Covent Garden (1630), thirty-one years; Bloomsbury (early eighteenth century), sixty-one years; Bloomsbury (end of eighteenth century), ninety-nine years. The average length of lease is ninety-nine years until the second half of the nineteenth century, and then it decreases. (Olsen, *ibid.*, pp. 29ff.)

16. *Ibid.*, p. 29.

17. Somers' Town was Lord Somers' private property; all landlords were not contemptuous of taking immediate profits. The characterization of Figs Mead is Olsen's. (*Ibid.*, p. 29.)

REGULARIZATION

18. Haussmann's use of the expression "régulariser" is to be found in his *Mémoires* (Paris: V. Havard, 1890–1893), Vol. III, pp. 67, 91, with regard to the parts of old Paris where he was establishing his new circulation system.

19. "Attila of the straight line" is to be found in Victor Fournel, *Paris nouveau et Paris futur* (Paris: Lecoffre, 1865), p. 220.

20. When offered the high position of Préfet de Police by the Emperor's envoy in 1851, Haussmann, then Préfet de Gironde, refused: "never in my life was I involved either in politics or even more in police affairs, unless duty bound. On the other hand, I have a deep relish for administration *per se;* it is my vocation." (Haussmann, *op cit.*, II, p. 8.)

21. The expressions appear in *Mémoires*, II, p. 200, excerpted by Haussmann from a speech of 1864.

22. Maurice Halbwachs, "Les plans d'extension et d'aménagement de Paris avant le XIXième siècle," in *La vie urbaine* (1920), p. 25.

23. The entire series of Balzac's *Comédie humaine* was published between 1830 and 1847 (*Le cousin Pons*), whereas Zola developed his Rougon-Macquarts cycle from 1871–1892. English industrial novels corresponding to Zola's phase are much earlier: *Mary Barton* was published in 1848, *Hard Times* in 1854.

24. In order, for instance, to avoid costly mistakes like the opening of the rue des Ecoles as had been ordered by Napoleon III.

25. Haussmann, *op. cit.*, III, pp. 424–425.

26. *Ibid.*, p. 50.

27. *Ibid.*, pp. 70, 90.

28. "It is presently the fashion among a group of archaeologists to admire without restraint the old Paris which they certainly never knew except through specialized books and collections of drawings..... They complain about the shameless stir of Baron Haussmann.... But they simply ignore the fact that the narrow winding streets of the center were practically impenetrable to traffic—dirty, stinking, and unhealthy.... Do show me a single monument, one artistic building which my administration destroyed (and did not help) to isolate." (*Ibid.*, p. 28.)

29. Brown, a gardener of genius (1716–1783) after the experiments of the early eighteenth century and notably Kent's attempt at the picturesque, arrived at the English natural garden based mostly on lineal composition and the contrast of "broad masses of light and shade, of lawn and tree." (Derek Clifford, *A History of Garden Design* [London: Faber and Faber, 1962].)

Paxton was also under the influence of Loudon, author of *Arboretum et Fruticetum Britannicum* (1838), who advocated artificiality and exoticism.

30. Frederick Law Olmsted, Jr., and Theodora Kimball, eds., *Frederick Law Olmsted, Landscape Architect, 1822–1903* (New York: G. P. Putnam's Sons, 1922–1928), p. 96. The reader is advised of a forthcoming book in the present series: Albert Fein, *Frederick Law Olmsted: A Design for the American City*.

31. "Twenty years hence the town will have enclosed Central Park. Let us consider, therefore, what will at that time be satisfactory, for it is then that the design will have to be really judged. No longer an open suburb, our ground will have around it a continuous high wall of bricks, stone, and marble." (Frederick Law Olmsted and Calvert Vaux, *Description of a Plan for the Improvement of the Central Park* [New York, 1858–1868], p. 8.)

32. This can be traced back to the vastness of wild spaces in America and in the case of Olmsted to the thousand-mile journeys by foot and on horseback during which he traversed the United States as far as California and Mexico. (See Olmsted and Kimball, *Frederick Law Olmsted*.)

33. *Ibid.*, p. 45.

34. See *Park Recreation Areas in the U.S.* (Washington, D.C.: U.S. Government Printing Office, 1928).

35. *Report from the Select Committee on Metropolitan Communications. Session 1854–55. Evidence of Sir Joseph Paxton*, p. 79, Qu 716 (7 June 1855).

36. The reading of this volume (which has not yet been translated) is, in spite of its length, fascinating. The equally large second volume contains only statistical data. The most recent study of Cerdá is by Arturo Soria y Puig in *Hogar y Arquitectura* (Madrid), No. 69, 1967, pp. 65ff.

37. See Vol. I, Book 4, Chap. 1, entitled "De la formación de las urbes, considerada bajo el punto de vista de las necessidades de cada época, de conformidad con los medios de locomoción de que en cada una de estas ha podido disponer el hombre." In the opening pages of his book, Cerdá gives a lively description of his emotion and wonder when he saw one of the first trains: he immediately sensed their importance for city planning.

38. Barthes' definition of metalanguage: "a system in which the content (as opposed to the expression) is itself formed by a system of meaning; in other words it is a semiotical system dealing with a semiotical system." ("Eléments de sémiologie" in *Communications* 4 [Paris: Le Seuil, 1964], p. 130.) I.e., metalanguage is used when one discusses language itself.
Compare with Cerdá's inventions the addiction of Patrick Geddes to coining new words such as *megalopolis, patholopolis, necropolis, politogenics, politopathy, paleo-* and *neo-technical, conurbation*, many of which have been adopted.

39. Note in particular the part played by Prosper Mérimée (1803–1870), who was nominated Inspecteur Général des monuments historiques in 1841.

PSEUDURBIAS AND REDUCED BEHAVIOR

40. The most complete, up-to-date analysis of these British efforts to be found is Walter Creese, *The Search for Environment: The Garden City Before and After* (New Haven: Yale University Press, 1966).

41. In particular, by Georges Benoit-Lévy, see *La Cité-jardin* (Paris: Henri Jouve, 1904).

PRE-URBANISM AND URBANISM: THE PROGRESSIST MODEL

42. The author has already used the terminology and concepts of *pré-urbanisme, progressisme, culturalisme* in *L'Urbanisme, utopies et réalites* (Paris: Le Seuil, 1965).

43. *Hygeia* (London: Macmillan & Co., 1876), p. 31.

44. While suppressing the differences which characterize syntagmatic association. See Note 4.

45. *Description du Phalanstère et considérations sur l'architectonique*, 2nd ed. (Paris: Librairie Sociétaire, 1848), p. 83.

46. Etienne Cabet, *Voyages et aventures de Lord William Carisdell en Icarie*, 2nd ed. (Paris: H. Souverain, 1842), p. 365.

47. See Anatole Kopp, *Ville et révolution* (Paris: Anthropos, 1967), which deals with architecture and city planning in the U.S.S.R. during the pre-Stalin years, from 1920 to the early thirties. (Forthcoming translation, as *Town and Revolution*, New York, George Braziller.)

48. *An Address Delivered to the Inhabitants of New Lanark, on the first of January 1816*, 3rd ed. (London, 1817), p. 11.

49. Le Corbusier wrote: "Tous les hommes ont mêmes organismes, mêmes fonctions. Tous les hommes ont les mêmes besoins." (All men have the same organisms and functions. All men have the same needs.) (*Vers une architecture* [Paris: Editions Crès, 1923], p. 108.) Again, for him man can be defined by "la somme des constantes psycho-sociologiques reconnues, inventoriées par des gens compétents." (The sum of a series of psycho-sociological constancies admitted and inventoried by competent people.) (*Manière de penser l'urbanisme* [1945], a series of articles republished by Gonthier, 1963, p. 38.)

50. Robert Owen had bought 30,000 acres of land. Three years later he had to sail back to England, having lost four fifths of his fortune.

51. In his first experience, Etienne Cabet had been joined by only seventy men for the exploitation of a thousand acres. In 1855 approximately a hundred people lived in Nauvoo, his second colony.

52. Godin has described the *familistère* in his very important book *Solutions sociales* published in 1870. R. H. Guerrand in *Les Origines du logement social en France* (Paris: Editions Ouvrières, 1967), pp. 160–166, which gives detailed information about Godin and his work, considers that Guise confronts us with the only true phalansteria experience, in spite of the charges of paternalism which were immediately made against it by contemporary socialists.

53. He had invented telegraphic apparatus and tried to have Madrid equipped with telephones and subways.

54. The first article is dated March 6, 1882, and the major one March 5, 1883.

55. George R. Collins and Carlos Flores, eds., *Arturo Soria y la Ciudad Lineal* (Madrid: Revista de Occidente, 1968), p. 37.

56. *Ibid.*, p. 16.

57. *Ibid.*, p. 35.

58. He gives it a value both biological and metaphysical: "The straight line, patroness and mate of a plan in all its details, represents perfection, convenience, riches, well-being, learning, and, indeed, the republic is a form of government." (Quoted by George Collins in *ibid.*, p. 18.) Soria will remain faithful to this position until the end of his life as evidenced by his *Ten Principles of Planning* of 1913. Compare Soria's valorization of the right angle to Le Corbusier's, especially in *Le Poème de l'angle droit* (Paris: Editions Verve, 1955).

59. *Vers une architecture*, pp. 38–39.

PRE-URBANISM AND URBANISM: THE CULTURALIST MODEL

60. Raymond Williams, (see Note 8), part I, chapters 1, 2, 4, 6, 7.

61. "Paris à vol d'oiseau," *Notre Dame de Paris* (Paris: Collection L'intégrale, Le Seuil), Vol. I, Book III, Chap. 2, pp. 286–287.

62. "Lectures on Architecture and Painting" delivered at Edinburgh in November, 1853. (London: Smith, Elder and Co., 1854, Lecture 1, p. 6).

63. *News from Nowhere* in *The Collected Works of William Morris* (London: Longmans, Green and Co., 1912), Vol. XVI.

64. *Art and Socialism* (1884), in *The Collected Works...*, Vol. XXIII, p. 204.

65. *How I Became a Socialist* (1894), in *The Collected Works...*, Vol. XXIII, pp. 279–281.

66. Camillo Sitte, *City Planning According to Artistic Principles*, translated by George R. Collins and Christiane Crasemann Collins (New York: Random House, 1965), pp. 4, 20.

67. *Ibid.*, p. 16.

68. *Ibid.*, p. 32.

69. Sitte explains his scheme in *ibid.*, chap. XII, "Example of an Urban Arrangement According to Artistic Principles."

70. For this residential suburb in Darmstadt see George R. and C. C. Collins, *Camillo Sitte and the Birth of Modern City Planning* (New York: Random House, 1965), fig. 16.

71. The Collinses showed how misleading C. Martin's translation was—chapter 7 was added entirely by the translator. Such alterations were even more damaging because, having no English version at their disposal, non-German architects and planners tended to read Sitte in the truncated French version.

72. See Charles Buls, *Esthétique des Villes* (Brussels: Buylant-Christophe, 1893) and "La conservation du coeur des anciennes villes," *Tekhne* (Brussels, 1912), nos. 64–66. In his Preface to *Esthétique*, Buls regrets the French deficiency in that field, and praises the German researches which, he says, were already numerous in 1860. He quotes in particular the names of Visschers, Botticher, Schnase, Lübke, Semper. At about the same time, Buls translated into French the first and up to now the only sample of Stübben's writings, a report to the International Engineering Conference in Chicago (1893), under the title: "La construction des villes. Règles pratiques et esthétiques à suivre pour l'élaboration des plans de villes" (Brussels: Lyon-Claesen, 1895). At the time of *Esthétique*, he seems to have been totally unaware of Sitte and his *Städte-Bau*.

73. Lewis Mumford, *The Culture of Cities* (New York: Harcourt, Brace, 1938), p. 24.

CONCLUSION

74. Geddes, a biologist, who suddenly had to change his career in 1878 because of a dramatic loss of visual acuity, which made microscopic research impossible, immediately approached sociological phenomenona in the light of Darwin. He himself declared that his method was directed against *utopian writing*.

75. See Kopp, *Ville et Révolution*, and Collins, "Linear Planning Throughout the World," *Journal of the Society of Architectural Historians*, XVIII (October, 1959); "Linear Planning," Dutch *Forum* (Amsterdam), XX–5 (March, 1968).

BIBLIOGRAPHY

BACKGROUND MATERIAL

The special, original character of city planning in industrial society and the break with tradition engendered by a new reflective approach toward planning can be fully grasped only in relation to other caesuras and transformations which occurred correspondingly during the nineteenth century. A complete list of works about economics, epistemology and technique would be too long, so we have made a selection of recommended titles.

Economics and Politics

Clapham, J. H. *An Economic History of Modern Britain.* Cambridge: The University Press, 1930–1938, 2 volumes.
———. *The Economic Development of France and Germany, 1815–1914.* Cambridge: The University Press, 1921.
Hacker, L. *The Triumph of American Capitalism.* New York: Simon and Schuster, 1940.
Morazé, C. *Les Bourgeois conquérants.* Paris: A. Colin, 1957.

Epistemology

Foucault, Michel. *Les mots et les choses.* Paris: Gallimard, 1965. An important work describing the transformations in the structure of Western thought since the sixteenth century, as observed in three key sectors: the theory of language, economics, and the natural sciences. The big break of the nineteenth century is clearly and forcefully defined.
Williams, Raymond. *Culture and Society, 1780–1950.* New York: Doubleday and Co., 1958; also published as paperback by Doubleday Anchor Books, 1959. Mainly concerned with Great Britain. Offers a stimulating description of a series of new concepts which accompanied the advent of industrial society.

A comparison between city planning in preindustrial and industrial society in many countries can be made initially with the help of the following general works:

Halbwachs, Maurice. *La population et les tracés de voirie à Paris.* Paris: Alcan, 1928.
———. "Les plans d'extension et d'aménagement de Paris avant le XIXième siècle," *La vie urbaine* (1920).
Hiorns, Frederick R. *Town Building in History.* London: George C. Harrap and Co., 1956. Well informed on Great Britain and the U.S. in the nineteenth century, but incomplete for other countries and periods.
Lavedan, Pierre. *Histoire de l'urbanisme.* Paris: Laurens, Vol. II, 1941, III, 1952. Incomplete from the point of view of concepts. Focused mainly on France. In spite of certain gaps, this is nonetheless a good complement to Mumford's works, due to numerous diagrams and extensive factual information.
Mumford, Lewis. *The Culture of Cities.* New York: Harcourt, Brace, 1938. Remains the most enlightening work insofar as it establishes the Industrial Revolution as the significant pivotal point.
Triggs, Inigo. *Town Planning, Past, Present and Possible.* London: Methuen, 1909. Clear and particularly interesting as a reflection of the point of view of a man who still belonged to the nineteenth century.

Concerning the specific subjects of our book, we have provided a bibliography by chapter. Only basic works have been included; others are in the Notes. A large number of writings by urbanists and contemporary texts have been included, and it is recommended that whenever possible the reader refer directly to these works.

THE CRITICAL ORDER

Urban sociology in the nineteenth century and the "clinical eye" (texts of the period)

Blanqui, A. J. *Les classes ouvrières en France pendant l'année 1848*. Paris: Didot, 1849, 2 vols. Part of the Petits Traités published by the Académie des Sciences Morales et Politiques.

Booth, Charles. *Life and Labour of the People in London*. London: MacMillan and Co., 1889–1902, 17 vols.

Chadwick, Edwin. *Report on the Sanitary Condition of the Labouring Population of Great Britain*. London: Her Majesty's Stationery Office, 1843.

————. *The Health of Nations*. A review of the works of Edwin Chadwick by B. W. Richardson. London: Longmans 1887, 2 vols.

Dodd, George. *Days at the Factories: or, the Manufacturing Industry of Great Britain Described*, Series I (London, 1843).

Engels, Friedrich. *Die Lage der arbeitenden Klasse in England*. Leipzig: Otto Wigand, 1845. English translation, *The Condition of the Working Class in England in 1844*, London, 1887.

Le Play, Frédéric. *Les ouvriers européens*. Paris: Imprimerie Imperiale, 1855.

Meuriot, P. *Des agglomérations urbaines de l'Europe contemporaine*. Paris: Belin Frères, 1897.

————. "Du concept de ville autrefois et aujourd'hui," *La Vie urbaine* (1919), p. 145. One of the best approaches to the semantic reduction experienced by large urban agglomerations during the nineteenth century.

Villermé, L. R. *Tableau de l'état physique et moral des ouvriers employés dans les manufactures de coton, de laine et de soie*. Paris: J. Renouard, 1840, 2 vols.

Weber, A. F. *The Growth of Cities in the Nineteenth Century*. New York: Mac-Millan, 1899; Cornell Reprints in Urban Studies, 1963.

The tradition of urban construction by English landlords

Olsen, Donald J. *Town-Planning in London, the Eighteenth and Nineteenth Centuries*. New Haven: Yale University Press, 1964.

Rasmussen, Steen Eiler. *London, the Unique City*. London: Jonathan Cape, 1937; Cambridge, Mass.: M.I.T. Press, 1967.

Summerson, Sir John. *Georgian London*. Baltimore, Md.: Penguin Books, 1962.

REGULARIZATION

Haussmann

Daly, César. "Les Travaux de Paris," *Revue générale de l'architecture* (Paris, 1862).

Fournel, Victor. *Paris nouveau et Paris futur*. Paris: Lecoffre, 1865. The critical outlook of a contemporary. The transition to a new order as perceived through a polemic, caricatural, but accurate vision.

Girard, Louis. *La politique des travaux publics du second Empire*. Paris: A. Colin, 1952.

Halbwachs, Maurice. *La population et les tracés de voirie à Paris*. Paris: Alcan, 1928.

————. "Les plans d'extension et d'aménagement de Paris avant le XIXième siècle," *La vie urbaine* (1920). In spite of the title and the fact that the author views Haussmann's plan as a pure *product* of collective needs, this brief article gives the clearest account of the Haussmann process and reveals its originality.

Haussmann, Baron Georges. *Mémoires*. Paris: V. Havard, 1890–1893, vols. See in particular the third volume for which Haussmann was correcting the proofs at the time of his death. This basic work is more valuable than the secondary studies of his work.

Attempts at regularization other than those by Haussmann, and the City considered as an Object (texts of the period)

Baumeister, R. *Stadterweiterungen in technischer, baupolizeilicher und wirtschaftlicher Beziehung*. Berlin: Ernst and Korn, 1876.

Cerdá, Ildefonso. *Teoría general de Urbanización*. Madrid, 1867, 2 vols.

Daly, César. "Comment les villes se sont formées," *Revue générale de l'architecture* (Paris, 1854).

Hénard, Eugène. *Études sur les transformations de Paris*. Paris: Librairies—Imprimeries réunies, 1903–1909. (See also Town Planning Conference, London, 1910, listed below under Pseudurbias and Reduced Behavior.)

Moore, Charles. *The Plan of Chicago by Daniel Burnham and Edward H. Bennet*. Chicago, 1909.

———. *Daniel Burnham, Architect Planner of Cities*. Boston and New York: Houghton Mifflin and Co., 1921, 2 vols.

Reichardt, Carl Friedrich. *Zur Bergründung einer allgemeinen Bauordnung in sanitäts sicherheits verkehres und ästhetischer Beziehung*. Hamburg: Meissner, 1863.

Stübben, J. *Der Städtebau*. Darmstadt: Bergstrasser, 1890.

———. "Der Bau der Städte in Geschichte und Gegenwart," *Centralblatt der Bauverwaltung*, XV (Berlin, 1895). See also *Second National Conference on City Planning & Congestion of Population at Rochester*, N. Y., May, 1910.

Wolf, Peter M. *Eugène Hénard and the Beginning of Urbanism in Paris 1900–1914*. Paris, 1968.

Paxton as a City Planner

Report from the Select Committee in Metropolitan Communications, Session 1854–1855, X.I (415).

Chadwick, George F. *The Works of Sir Joseph Paxton*. London: The Architectural Press, 1961. A basic work containing a detailed analysis of the various facets of the personality of a man whose name is too often connected solely with the Crystal Palace.

Olmsted and the American Park System

Fein, Albert, ed. *Landscape into Cityscape; Frederick Olmsted's Plans for a Greater New York City*. Ithaca: Cornell University Press, 1967.

Olmsted, Frederick Law. "Park," *New American Cyclopedia of Appleton*. New York, 1860.

———. *Public Parks & the Enlargement of Town*. Cambridge, Mass., 1870.

———, and Calvert Vaux. *Description of a Plan for the Improvement of the Central Park*. New York, 1858–1868.

Olmsted, Frederick Law, Jr., and Theodora Kimball, eds. *Frederick Law Olmsted, Landscape Architect, 1822–1903*. New York and London: G. P. Putnam's Sons, 1922–1928, 2 vols. Frederick Law Olmsted, Jr., collaborated with his father and later became his successor. The book contains a number of quotations from the writings of Frederick Law Olmsted.

PSEUDURBIAS AND REDUCED BEHAVIOR

Dyos, H. J. *Victorian Suburb*. Leicester: University Press, 1961.

Guerrand, R. H. *Les origines du logement social en France*. Paris: Editions Ouvrières, 1967. Thorough review of the situation in France. Contains an excellent bibliography.

Meakin, Bridgett. *Model Factories & Villages*. London: T. Fisher Unwin, 1905.

Mielke, Robert. "Die Entwicklung der dörflichen Siedlungen und ihrer Beziehungen zum Städtebau alter und neuer Zeit," *Der Städtebau*, VI (1913), no. 5. See also G. Duveau in Note 6.

PRE-URBANISM AND URBANISM: THE PROGRESSIST MODEL

Pre-urbanism

Texts

Bellamy, E. *Looking Backward*. Boston, 1888; republished, 1931.

Borie, Henry Jules. *Aérodomes, essai sur un nouveau mode d'habitation*. Paris: Imprimerie de Morris, 1865.

Buckingham, James S. *National Evils & Practical Remedies, with the Plan of a Model Town*. London: Peter Jackson, 1849.

Cabet, Etienne. *Voyages et aventures de Lord William Carisdall en Icarie*. Paris: H. Souverain, 1840.

———. *Colonie icarienne aux Etats-Unis*. Paris, by the author, 1856.

Considérant, Victor. *Description du Phalanstère*. Paris, Librairie sociétaire, 1840.

———. *Exposition abregée du système phalanstérien de Fourier*. Paris: Librairie sociétaire, 1845.

Fourier, Charles. *Cités ouvrières. Des modifications à introduire dans l'architecture des villes.* Paris, Librairie phalanstérienne, 1849 (written in 1820).

―――. *Traité de l'association domestique.* Paris: Bossange Père, 1822.

―――. *Le nouveau monde industriel et sociétaire.* Paris: Bossange Père, 1829.

Mathieu, A. *Projet d'une Capitale modèle.* Paris: J. Baudry, 1880.

Owen, Robert. *A New View of Society.* London: Cadell and Davies, 1813.

―――. *A new View of Society and Other Writings (with an Introduction by G. D. H. Cole).* London and Toronto: J. M. Dent and Sons; New York: E. P. Dutton and Co., 1927. Contains a critical anthology of Owen's major writings.

―――. *The Book of the New Moral World.* London: E. Wilson, 1836.

―――. *An Address Delivered to the Inhabitants of New Lanark.* London: Longman, Hurst, Rees, Orme, Brown, 1817.

Richardson, Benjamin Ward. *Hygeia, A City of Health.* London: MacMillan, 1876.

Critical Works

Choay, Françoise. *L'Urbanisme, utopies et réalites.* Paris: Le Seuil, 1965.

Conrads, Ulrich, and Hans G. Sperlich, *The Architecture of Fantasy: Utopian Building and Planning in Modern Times* (translated and adapted by C. C. and G. R. Collins). New York: Frederick A. Praeger, 1963.

Mumford, Lewis. *The Story of Utopia.* London: G. G. Harrap & Co., 1923; new edition, New York: The Viking Press, 1962.

Riesman, O. "Some Observations on Community Plans & Utopias," *Yale Law Journal* (December, 1947).

Urbanism

Texts

Benoit-Lévy, Georges. *La cité-jardin.* Paris: Henri Jouve, 1904. A progressist version of the English culturalist idea.

Soria y Mata, Arturo. *La Ciudad Lineal, Antecedentes y datos varios acerca de su construcción.* Madrid: Est Tipográfico "Succesores de Rivadenegra," 1894. (See also *La Ciudad Lineal*, a review published from 1897).

Garnier, Tony. *Une cité industrielle, étude pour la construction des villes.* Paris: Vincent, 1917. Illustrated with plates exhibited at the Academy from 1904 on. Unfortunately it is now very difficult to find. But see the following title appearing in the present series of books: Wiebenson, Dora. *Tony Garnier: the Cité Industrielle.* New York: George Braziller, 1969.

Pawlowski, Christophe. *Tony Garnier et les débuts de l'urbanisme fonctionnel en France.* Paris, 1967.

Town Planning Conference, London, 1910, *Transactions*, London, R.I.B.A., 1911.

Critical Works

Collins, George R. "Linear Planning throughout the World," *Journal of the Society of Architectural Historians*, XVIII (October, 1959).

―――, and Carlos Flores, eds. *Arturo Soria y la Ciudad Lineal.* Madrid: Revista de Occidente, 1968. A basic work on Soria and linear planning, with most of his writings.

Giedion, Sigfried. *Space, Time and Architecture.* Cambridge: Harvard University Press, 1941; revised edition, 1967.

Jürgens, Oskar. *Spanische Städte, ihre bauliche Entwicklung, und Ausgestaltung.* Hamburg, 1926.

Zevi, Bruno. *Storia dell'architettura modernà.* Torino: Einaudi, 1950.

PRE-URBANISM AND URBANISM: THE CULTURALIST MODEL

Pre-urbanism

Howard, Ebenezer. *To-morrow, a Peaceful Path to Social Reform.* London: Swan Sonnenschein & Co., 1898. New edition with preface and introduction by F. J. Osborn and Lewis Mumford, London, Faber & Faber, 1946.

Morris, William. *The Collected Works of William Morris.* London: Longmans, Green and Co. Vol. XVI, 1912: *News from Nowhere;* Vol. XXII, 1914: *Hopes & Fears for Art. Lectures on Art & Industry.*

Ruskin, John. *The Seven Lamps of Architecture.* London: Smith, Elder and Co., 1849.

―――. *The Stones of Venice.* London: Smith, Elder and Co., 1851–1853, 3 vols (see particularly vol. 2, chap. 6).

―――. *The Crown of Wild Olive.* London: Smith, Elder and Co., 1866.

Texts:

Buls, Charles. *Esthétique des villes*. Brussels: Buylant-Christophe, 1893.

———. "La conservation du coeur des anciennes villes," *Tekhne*, nos. 64–66 (Brussels, 1912).

Fischer, Theodor. *Sechs Vorträge über Stadtbaukunst*. Munich: Oldenbourg, 1919.

Henrici, Karl. "Langweilige und Kurzweilige Strassen," *Deutsche Bauzeitung*, XXVII (1893).

———. "Zür schönheitlichen Gestaltung städtischer Strassen," *Deutsche Bauzeitung*, XXVII (1893).

———. "Camillo Sitte als Begründer einer neuen Richtung im Städtebau," *Zeitschrift des Österreichischen Ingenieur und Architekten Vereins*, LVI (1904).

Horsfall, Thomas. *The Improvement of the Dwellings and Surroundings of the People: the Example of Germany*. Manchester: University Press, 1904. Work responsible for the propagation of Sitte's ideas in Great Britain.

Sitte, Camillo. *Der Städte-Bau nach seinen künsterischen Grundsätzen*. Vienna: Carl Graeser, 1889.

———. *City Planning According to Artistic Principles*, translated by G. R. Collins and C. C. Collins. New York: Random House, 1965. First complete and critical English translation.

———. *L'art de bâtir les villes*, translated by Camille Martin. Geneva and Paris, 1902 (and 1918). Not to be consulted without bearing in mind certain precautions indicated by Collins in *Camillo Sitte and the Birth of Modern City Planning*, see below.

Unwin, Raymond. *Town Planning in Practice, an Introduction to the Art of Designing Cities & Suburbs*. London: Unwin, 1909.

Der Städtebau, a periodical first put out in 1904 by Theodor Goecke and Camillo Sitte.

Town Planning Conference, London, 1910 (see above).

Critical Works

Ashworth, William. *The Genesis of Modern British Town Planning*. London: Routledge & Kegan Paul, 1954.

Collins, George R., and C. C. Collins. *Camillo Sitte and the Birth of Modern City Planning*. New York: Random House, 1965. Contains notes on the translation of *Der Städte-Bau* (*City Planning According to Artistic Principles*) mentioned above. Establishes Sitte in the context of his period. Contains a valuable bibliography which covers not only the entire Sittesque movement but all the trends in German city planning during the second half of the nineteenth century.

Macfadyen, Dugald. *Sir Ebenezer Howard and the Town Planning Movement*. Manchester: University Press, 1933.

Eden, W. A. "Studies in Urban Theory II," in *Town Planning Review*, XIX (1947). The sources of Howard, especially Buckingham.

CONCLUSION

Survey and Urban Geography

Geddes, Patrick. *Cities in Evolution: an Introduction to the Town Planning Movement & to the Study of Civics*. London: Williams and Norgate, 1915.

———. *City Development; a Study of Paris, Gardens and Culture-Institutes, A Report to the Carnegie Dumferline Trust*. Edinburgh and Westminster: Geddes and Co., 1904.

Mairet, P. *A Pioneer of Sociology, the Life & Letters of Patrick Geddes*. London: Lund Humphries, 1957.

Ratzel, F. *Anthropo-Geographie*. Stuttgart: J. Engelhorn, 1882.

Reclus, Elisée. "The Evolution of Cities," *The Contemporary Review* (February, 1895).

City Exhibitions

Ratzel, F., K. Bücher, G. von Mayr, H. Waentig, G. Simmel, Th. Petermann, and D. Schäfer. *Die Grosstadt, Vorträge und Aufsätze zur Städte Ausstellung*. Dresden, 1903.

Führer durch die allgemeine Städtebau-Ausstellung in Berlin, 1910. Berlin: Wasmuth, 1910.

Hegemann, Werner. *Der Städtebau nach den Ergebnissen der allgemeinen Städtebau-Ausstellung in Berlin 1910*. Berlin: Wasmuth, 1911–1913, 2 vols. With a culturalist tendency.

CHRONOLOGICAL CHART*

City Planning	Mathematics, Natural Sciences and Applications	Philosophy and Social Sciences
1765 Beginning of the transformation of St. Petersburg	(1774) **Steam Engine developed by Watt**	
1767 Royal Crescent, Bath James Craig's plan for the extension of Edinburgh		
1769 Patte: *Mémoire sur les objets les plus importants de l'architecture*	**First steam automobile, by Cugnot**	
1771 Blondel: *Cours d'Architecture*		
1773 Ledoux's project for the town of Chaux		
1775	Volta: electrophorus Lavoisier: theory of oxidation	
1776 Bedford Square, London Beginning of the upper town in Brussels		Adam Smith: *Inquiry into the Nature & Causes of the Wealth of Nations*
1781	**First aeronautic trip with the Montgolfier balloon**	
1783		Kant: *Kritik der reinen Vernunft*
1784	Cort: puddling	
1785	Lavoisier: *Mémoire sur la respiration* Cartwright: mechanical loom	
1788	Lagrange: *Méchanique Analytique*	
1789 L'Enfant's plan for Washington D.C.		
1791 Robert Adam, Charlotte Square, Edinburgh		
1793 Plan for Paris known as the Artists' Plan		
1794		Condorcet: *Esquisse d'un tableau historique des progrès de l'esprit humain*

*N.B. This chart is not complete. Our purpose is not to catalog all the major events of the nineteenth century but to indicate a certain number of *correlations*. First a correlation existing between the semantical impoverishment undergone by nineteenth-century cities and the development of a new and more efficient, rapid systems of information and communication which replaced the semiotic urban system. Secondly, a correlation between the advent of critical planning and the evolution of new concepts and of new methods in science and philosophy. Finally, a correlation between the metalanguages of critical urban planning and the theoretical language used in natural and biological sciences. In some instances, especially from the 1880's on, the absence of any correlation has been noted as well.

The size of this book does not permit a complete chart, with a fourth column indicating artistic developments (plastic arts and literature). Therefore, this column, which, however instructive, would have been less directly related to the subject of our book, has been omitted.

Italics indicate book titles. **Bold face** type indicates events or inventions directly related to communication and information.

City Planning	Mathematics, Natural Sciences and Applications	Philosophy and Social Sciences
1797		Schelling: *Ideen zur einer Naturphilosophie*
1798		Malthus: *An Essay on the Principle of Population*
1800		
1804 Ledoux: *L'Architecture , considérée sous le rapport de l'art, des moeurs et de la législation*	**First trip made by Thevithick's first train locomotive**	
1806 Repton: *Enquiry into the Changes of Taste in Land- scape Gardening* First section of the rue de Rivoli		
1807		Hegel: *Phänomenologie des Geistes*
1809	Lamarck: *Philosophie Zoologique*	
1812 (−1827) Nash: Regent Street and Regent's Park	Laplace: *Théorie analytique des probabilités*	Hegel: *Wissenschaft des Logik*
1813 Owen: *A New View of Society*		
1816	G. Cuvier: *Le règne animal distribué d'après son organisation* **The Times, steam printed**	F. Bopp: *Über das Konjugations- system der Sanskritsprache*
1817		D. Ricardo: *Principles of Political Economy and Taxation*
1818	Cauchy: *Cours d'Analyse de l'Ecole Polytechnique*	Schopenhauer: *Die Welt als Wille* J. Grimm: *Deutsche Grammatik*
1821 (−1822)	J. Fourier: analytic theory of heat	Champollion: *Lettre à Monsieur Dacier, relative à l'alphabet des hiéroglyphes*
1824	N. Niepce: **first photography** Sadi Carnot: Second Principle of thermodynamics	
1825	**First train owned by a private company is drawn by Stephenson's steam engine**	
1828	F. Woehler: synthesis of urea	
1829 Fourier: *Le nouveau monde industriel et sociétaire*	Stephenson: construction of *The Rocket*	
1830 Foundation of *Inspection des Monuments Historiques*	**Inauguration of the first modern railway line, Liverpool–Manchester; The Rocket, 32 kilometers per hour** Foundation of the Krupp factories	
1835	Gauss: **electric telegraph (presented to the Saxon railways)**	
1836 Owen: *The Book of the New Moral World*		Grotefend: *Beiträge zur Erläute- rung der Persepolitanischen Keilschrift*
1837 Foundation of Adelaide, Australia		

City Planning	Mathematics, Natural Sciences and Applications	Philosophy and Social Sciences
1839	Schwann: cellular theory	Auguste Comte: *Cours de Philosophie positive*
1840 Cabet: *Voyage en Icarie*		
1841		Feuerbach: *Das Wesen des Christentums*
1842 Chadwick: *Report on the Sanitary Condition of the Labouring People of Great Britain*		
1843	**First telegraph office opened in Great Britain**	
1844 Paxton: beginning of Birkenhead; *Reports of the Royal Commission On the State of Large Towns & Populus Districts* (44–45)		A. Comte: *Discours sur l'esprit positif*
1845		Engels: *Die Lage der arbeitenden Klasse in England*
1847 Salt Lake City, Utah		
1848 Public Health Act		Marx and Engels: *Das Manifest des Kommunisten*
1849 Buckingham: *National Evils and Practical Remedies* Ruskin: *The Seven Lamps of Architecture*		
1851 Paxton: Crystal Palace (International Exhibition in London)		
1852 Titus Salt: Saltaire (Yorkshire)		
1853 Haussmann appointed Prefect of the Seine	**First elevator in New York**	
1854 Haussmann's plan for Paris, first thoroughfares First project for the Metropolitan Railway, London	R. Riemann: *Über die Hypothese Welche die Geometrie zu Grunde Liegen* G. Boole: *An Investigation of the Laws of Thought*	T. Mommsen: *Römische Geschichte* (beginning)
1855 Paxton: The Great Victorian Way	(1877) Bessemer Process	Humboldt: *Cosmos*
1857 Olmsted and Vaux: plan for Central Park Le Vésinet		
1859 Cerdá's plan for Barcelona Plan for Vienna ratified by Franz-Joseph *Familistère* at Guise	Darwin: *The Origin of Species*	
1860	**Combustion engine**	Schleicher: *Abrégé de Grammaire comparée des langues indo-germaniques* J. Burckhardt: *Die Kultur der Renaissance in Italien*
1861	**Asphalt**	Fechner: *Elemente*
1862 Right Bank circle railway in Paris		Spencer: *Principles*

City Planning	Mathematics, Natural Sciences and Applications	Philosophy and Social Sciences
1863 London Underground Railway	Maxwell theory of the electric field	
1864	The Martin oven	Fustel de Coulanges: *La cité antique*
1865	G. Mendel: birth of genetics F. A. Kekulé: structure of benzene Maxwell: theory of the propagation of electro-magnetic waves	
1866	**First transatlantic cable**	
1867 Cerdá: *Teoría general de Urbanización*	**Marinoni rotary printing press**	Marx: *Das Kapital* (first book)
1868		
1869	Mendeleev: classification of the elements	Schliemann: *Ithaka*
1870	**Balloon postal service during the siege of Paris**	
1871		E. B. Tylor: *Primitive Culture*
1872	F. Klein: *Erlanger Programm*	
1874 Obligatory building program for all Swedish municipalities		
1876 Richardson: *Hygeia*	Bell: **telephone**	
1877 Shaw: Bedford Park Morris: Society for the Protection of Ancient Buildings	Pasteur: origin of infectious diseases Claude Bernard: *Leçons sur les phénomènes de la vie commune aux animaux et aux végétaux*	
1878	Edison: incandescent light bulb **phonograph**	F. de Saussure: *Mémoire sur le système primitif des voyelles dans les langues indo-européennes*
1879 Bournville, England		Le Play: *La méthode sociale* Nietzsche: *Human, all too Human*
1880 Pullman City, U.S.A. Agneta Park, Delft		
1882 Soria: La Ciudad Lineal (in *El Progreso*)	Deprez: **first long-distance transmission of power by electric current**	Nietzsche: *Die fröhliche Wissenschaft* Bakunin: *God and the State*
1884 Foundation of Johannesburgh		Mommsen: *Römische Geschichte* (end)
1887	**Automatic telephone**	
1888 Port Sunlight, England		
1889 Creation of the London County Council Sitte: *Der Städte-Bau nach seinen künstlerischen Grundsätze*	**First automobile** Branly: **principle of the radio** H. Hertz: generalization of the electro-magnetic wave theory Elster and Geitel: **photoelectric cell**	Nietzsche: *Götzen Dämmerung*
1890 Henrici: plan for the extension of Dessau Morris: *News from Nowhere*		

124

City Planning	Mathematics, Natural Sciences and Applications	Philosophy and Social Sciences
1893 Parliamentary decision to abolish the gates of London Burnham, Olmsted, et al.: setting up of international exhibition in Chicago	C. Jordan: *Traité d'Analyse* (2nd ed.) **Diesel engine**	
1894 Beginning of the Ciudad Lineal in Madrid Alfredshof, Krupp Colony	H. Hertz: *Die Prinzipien der Mechanik*	
1895	Lumière Brothers: **movies** Popov: **first radio tests** G. Cantor: *Beiträge zur Begründung der Transfinition Mengenlehre*	
1896 Otto Wagner: *Moderne Architektur*	Becquerel: radioactivity W. K. Roentgen: X-rays	Pareto: *Cours d'économie politique*
1897 Foundation of the review *La Ciudad Lineal*	J. J. Thomson: the electron Buchner: enzymes Apel and Crawford: extraction of adrenalin	
1898 Howard: *To-morrow: Peaceful Path to Real Reform*		
1899 Association of the Garden Cities of London		
1900	D. Hilbert: *Grundlagen der Geometrie* Max Planck: quantum theory	Freud: *Traumdeutung*
1901		Husserl: *Logische Untersuchungen*
1903 Letchworth City Planning Exhibition in Dresden	**First airplane flight**	Lenin: *What Is To Be Done*
1904 Geddes: Plan for Dumfermline, Scotland *City Development* Garnier's Exhibition of the cité industrielle		Max Weber: *Die protestantische Ethik und der Geist des Kapitalismus*
1905 Krupp Colony Margaretenhof	Einstein: *Zur Elektrodynamik bewegter Körper* Photo-electric effect	Cassirer: *Das Erkenntnis-Problem*
1906		Bergson: *l'Evolution créatrice*
1907 Unwin: Hampstead Garden Suburb	L. de Forest: trioae lamp	
1909 Unwin: *Town Planning in Practice* Hellerau: first German Garden City Town and Country Planning Act		
1910 City Planning Exhibition in Berlin First International Conference on City Planning in London	Whitehead and Russell: *Principia Mathematica*	
1911		F. Boas: *Handbook of American Indian Languages*
1912	Niels Bohr: model of the atom	
1915 Geddes: *Cities in Evolution*		Wölfflin: *Kunstgeschichte Grundbegriffe*
1916	Einstein: *Die Grundlagen der allgemeinen Relativität*	F. de Saussure: *Cours de linguistique générale*

INDEX

SOURCES OF ILLUSTRATIONS

We gratefully acknowledge the services of Jacques Ostier, Paris, the picture researcher who gathered most of the photographic material for this book.

Jean Alphand, *Les Promenades de Paris* (Paris, 1867–1873): 22

Architectural Review (April, 1943): 66

Stewart Bale Ltd., Liverpool: 38

Edward Beeson, *Port Sunlight* (New York, 1911): 48

Bibliothèque Nationale, Paris: 2, 3, 6, 9, 10, 13, 23, 25, 29, 35, 43, 46, 57, 58, 60; *R. Ackermann's Repository of Arts* (1822): 7; Jean Alphand, *Les Promenades de Paris:* 24; *Colton's General Atlas with Descriptions* (New York, 1857): 36, 37; Tony Garnier, *Une Cité Industrielle* (Lyon, 1919): 67, 68, 69; Jean-Baptiste Godin, *Solutions Sociales* (Paris, 1871); 61; Eugène Hénard, *Les Transformations de Paris* (1903): 26, 27; Krupp, *Evolution des colonies de travailleurs:* 50, 51, 52, 53; *The Life of Robert Owen* (London, 1858): 55; Donald J. Olsen, *Town Planning in London* (New Haven, 1964): 12; J. Stübben, *Der Städtebau* (Darmstadt, 1890): 4, 11, 28, 33, 34, 54; *Les Travaux de Paris 1789–1889* (Paris): 20, 21; Raymond Unwin, *Etude pratique du plan des villes* (London, 1930): 42, 76, 79, 80, 81

The Bournville Village Trust 1900–1955 (Bournville, 1955): 48

Philippe Brossé, Paris, provided photographs for the following: 2, 3, 4, 5, 6, 7, 9, 10, 11, 12, 13, 14, 16, 17, 18, 19, 21, 23, 24, 25, 26, 27, 28, 29, 32, 33, 34, 35, 36, 37, 42, 43, 46, 47, 50, 51, 52, 53, 54, 55, 58, 60, 61, 67, 68, 69, 76, 79, 80, 81

Chiswick District Library, London: 44

Collection Yvan Christ, Paris: 18

Commercial Club, Chicago: 38

Frederick Gibberd, *Town Design* (New York, 1967): 45

Cornelius Gurlitt, *Zur Befreiung der Baukunst* (Ullstein, 1968): 8

André Gutton, *Conversations sur l'architecture*, VI (Paris, 1962): 59

Ebenezer Howard, *Garden Cities of To-morrow* (London, 1965): 77, 78

Instituto Municipal de Historia, Barcelona: 30, 31

Collection André Jauives, Paris: 47

Musée Kodak, Collection Chasseau-Flaviers, Paris: 32

Courtesy of the New-York Historical Society, New York City: 40, 56

The New York Public Library, Map Division, Astor, Lenox and Tilden Foundations: 15

Parliamentary Papers, Report of the Select Committee on Metropolitan Communications (1854–1855): 41

John Reps, *The Making of Urban America* (Princeton, 1965): 1

John Ruskin, *The Poetry of Architecture* (New York, 1873): 70

Collection Georges Sirot, Paris: 5, 14, 16, 17, 19

Camillo Sitte, *City Planning According to Artistic Principles* (New York, 1965): 71, 72, 73, 74, 75

Arturo Soria y Hernandez, *The Problem of Land in Spain* (Madrid, 1926): 62, 63, 64, 65